Praise

'I loved this! Lisa has X-ray vision into a person's mind and soul. What she sees and articulates about why we do what we do makes for such a fascinating read.'
   — **John Patrick Morgan**, Founder, Creating, and TEDx speaker

'Lisa's book is the *very* best combination of workbook and book – she walks us through the different ways we can look at life and how to maximise both our experience of life and the results we get, inside and out. Lisa invites us to ask deep questions of ourselves and dig deep in service to creating the life we want. This book will serve *you* – and it will serve anyone you give it to.'
   — **Carolyn Freyer-Jones**, Professional Coach, CFJ Coaching Success School

'This book stands apart from other transformational reads, with Lisa's brilliance as a coach shining through every page. Her perspective is refreshingly direct, presenting new yet often simple insights and concepts that spark light bulb moments throughout. This book is destined to become an indispensable resource for anyone who reads it, promising lasting, life-changing impact for all.'
   — **Kate Williams**, Communications Strategist and former Head of Press, ITV Channels

'What I love about Lisa's approach is she holds up a mirror and asks us what we see. No running, no dodging – just the hard questions that offer truth and motivation as a path forward. Just enough coaching, tools and inspiration to get you where you've always wanted to go.'
　　— **Jesse Lipscombe**, best-selling author, actor, speaker and activist

'If you're wanting to think bigger, this book is for you. It's full of Lisa's enthusiasm around how we can change our lives, starting with our thoughts, and has lots of practical activities and case studies to support you. I highly recommend reading it. You will be different by the end of this book.'
　　— **Ruth Kudzi**, Master Certified Coach (MCC), Optimus Coach Academy

'This book will refine your approach to challenges, strengthen your decision making and help you lead with clarity and perspective. Lisa has a gift for blending knowledge and wisdom alongside practical application. Her approach is both relatable and transformative, making this book impactful on many levels. For anyone wanting to break through personal or professional limits, the wisdom in here will guide you to deep insight and help you turn aspiration into action.'
　　— **Nick Kewney**, Co-Founder and CPTO, Layer Systems

TRULY YOU

AN INVITATION TO BE
MORE OF YOUR TRUE SELF

Lisa Hopper

Re think

First published in Great Britain in 2025
by Rethink Press (www.rethinkpress.com)

© Copyright Lisa Hopper

All rights reserved. No part of this publication may be reproduced, stored in or introduced into a retrieval system, or transmitted, in any form, or by any means (electronic, mechanical, photocopying, recording or otherwise) without the prior written permission of the publisher.

The right of Lisa Hopper to be identified as the author of this work has been asserted by her in accordance with the Copyright, Designs and Patents Act 1988.

This book is sold subject to the condition that it shall not, by way of trade or otherwise, be lent, resold, hired out, or otherwise circulated without the publisher's prior consent in any form of binding or cover other than that in which it is published and without a similar condition including this condition being imposed on the subsequent purchaser.

*To my family, for your unwavering
love, support and encouragement*

Contents

Foreword   1

Introduction   5
   You don't get what you want,
   you get who you're being   6
   How to get the most from this book   11

PART ONE   A Fresh Understanding   15

1   The Big Illusion   17
   Advice for my younger self   18
   The nature of thought – the simplest
   route to peace and happiness   21
   Key insights   29

2   It's An Inside Job   31
   The heart's barometer   32
   Outside-in vs inside-out living   36
   The voice of the ego mind   37
   The operating system   39
   Witness consciousness   44
   Key insights   45

3	**Thought Is A Superpower**	**47**
	Thought is not the enemy	48
	Your unique curriculum	51
	Embracing the mystery of the unknown	52
	Our growth areas	56
	Key insights	61
4	**Your Powerful Ally**	**63**
	Black dot vs white space	63
	Learning to surrender	65
	Key insights	71
5	**Iceberg Right Ahead!**	**73**
	Meet your subconscious mind	73
	Question your beliefs	76
	Explore your roots	78
	The road ahead	80
	Don't surrender your truth, surrender to your truth	82
	Key insights	85

PART TWO   Thirteen Life Lessons That Change The Game   **89**

Lesson 1   The Game Is Played And Won On The Court, Not From The Spectator Stand   **91**
   Read for information, inhabit for transformation   91
   Live your dreams   92
   An understanding always at work   93
   Key insights   99

Lesson 2   Be The Creator, Not The Victim   **101**
   Embracing the future   101

Removing the ceiling	106
Key insights	108

Lesson 3 Becoming Lucky — **111**
Are you resistant to being lucky?	111
How luck matters	115
Key insights	117

Lesson 4 What Is Here Vs What We Think Is Here Vs What We Think About What We Think Is Here — **119**
A fresh look at gratitude	120
Higher vibes	123
Key insights	126

Lesson 5 You Are The Loving Witness, Not The Thought — **129**
Can we control our thoughts?	129
The gift of free will	131
Key insights	136

Lesson 6 Identifying Secondary Gains — **137**
Hidden influences	137
Key insights	143

Lesson 7 Integrity To Your Word (And The Prison Where You Hold The Key) — **145**
The importance of integrity	146
The prison of integrity	150
Honouring vs keeping your word	150
When integrity can stop you from making a commitment	151
You are always in integrity with something	155
Key insights	156

**Lesson 8   Your Judgements On Others Are
  Keeping You Stuck** **159**
   When we judge others most   159
   Why we judge others   161
   How to turn this around   164
   Key insights   166

Lesson 9   Forgiveness **169**
   Accepting new perspectives   170
   Learning to forgive   171
   Apologies   175
   When it's hard to forgive   177
   Key insights   180

**Lesson 10   Tolerating Truth And Radical
  Self-Love** **183**
   Understanding our untruths   184
   Achieving new heights   185
   Adding the fun factor   187
   Finding your true potential   187
   Key insights   191

**Lesson 11   Upgrade Your Questions,
  Upgrade Your Life** **193**
   What makes a question carry
   so much gravitas?   198
   The double-edged sword of strengths   199
   Being open to change   200
   Key insights   202

Lesson 12   Allow Everything, Accommodate Little **205**
   Defining unconditional love   206
   Creating boundaries   207

Navigating boundaries	209
Key insights	213

Lesson 13 The Six-Year-Old In The Boardroom Of Your Life — 215

An outdated view of ourselves	216
The consequences of both change and staying still	217
Rewiring for success	218
What successful people know	219
The power of choice	220
How does our younger self impact our current life subconsciously?	222
Key insights	224

PART THREE An Invitation To Your Life 2.0 — 227

An Invitation To... Be Your Future Self Now — 229

Shifting our mindset	230
Stepping into our future self	234

An Invitation To... Embrace Radical Authenticity — 239

Stepping out of the familiar	239
Why we accept our labels	242
Time to switch it up	243

An Invitation To... Make Your Mission Bigger Than Your Fears — 245

Overcoming barriers	245

An Invitation To... Acknowledge The Gain — 251

Shifting our perceptions	252
Unlocking our potential	253

An Invitation To... Make Powerful,
Meaningful Commitments — **259**
    Make your commitments — 261
    Some good reminders — 263
    Words of encouragement — 264

It's A Wrap! — **267**

Acknowledgements — **271**

Lisa's 'Little Gems, Big Impact' — **275**

The Author — **277**

Foreword

There are plenty of self-help books out there, but *Truly You* isn't just another one of them. Lisa Hopper didn't write this book to feed you feel-good platitudes or offer empty promises of overnight success. What you'll find here is a real, raw, direct and practical guide to becoming who you really are and creating a life that aligns with your highest potential.

Lisa and I go way back. I've seen her evolve, not just as a coach but as someone who lives the principles she teaches. She knows, like few others do, that transformation doesn't come from simply 'thinking positively' or making superficial changes. Real change, lasting profound change, comes from a deep understanding of who you are at your core and from challenging everything you thought you knew about yourself, and then stepping into action. This is what makes Lisa a force to be reckoned with in the coaching world.

Lisa brings her straight-talking style to the page. She has a unique way of embodying powerful love while simultaneously calling you out and not sugar coating anything. She talks about dialling up the love in the container so it can handle the heat. That is what she does in *Truly You*. Lisa knows the people who will benefit from this book don't need fluff – they need honesty, clarity and action. This book is designed to strip away the layers of self-doubt, limiting beliefs and social conditioning that have held you back. It's an invitation to drop the mask, embrace radical authenticity and build a life that is more in alignment with your true self.

What sets her apart as a coach, and what makes this book so powerful, is her ability to connect the dots between mindset and action. She doesn't just show you how to shift your thinking, she shows you how to translate those shifts into real-world results. The thirteen life lessons along with the five invitations she outlines in this book are simple yet profound. They'll challenge you, push you, and, if you let them, transform you.

Lisa's clients experience breakthroughs that have changed their lives. This book offers you the same opportunity but only if you're willing to get real with yourself and do the work. If you're ready to stop playing small, get unstuck and create a life that reflects the real you, then this is the book that will take you there.

FOREWORD

Lisa Hopper is the coach who helps people make extraordinary leaps, and this book is a testament to that. Read it, apply it and watch what happens.

Michael Serwa
Coach for the Elite

Introduction

Most of us are asleep to who we are being. We bop about our lives on autopilot, following the habitual, subconscious programming we inherited from a young age – conditioning we have come to believe we are. We *say* we want change, but our actions continue to align with our old patterns of behaviour, rather than what we say we want. Rarely do we stop to take a closer look at what is driving those patterns. This book is here to help wake you from your slumber, release what no longer serves you, and reconnect you to your power within. All of this, in service of your fullest, most aligned and authentic life yet.

You don't get what you want, you get who you're being

I have worked with hundreds of individuals over the years on understanding more about our true nature, while simultaneously shedding the limitations of their learned conditioning. Time and time again, I have seen them make significant and sustainable change in their lives. Change that they previously did not think possible for them.

I have watched people from all walks of life – business owners, entrepreneurs, leaders, creatives and everyday changemakers – discover and bring alive the impact and contribution they have longed to make. I have seen each person stepping into a more fully expressed version of themselves, created from a new understanding of who they are. An understanding that allows them to amplify their impact, their contribution and their results.

Some of those people have left the shackles of their long-term corporate jobs; some have started and scaled their businesses. Others have gained promotions beyond what they thought they were capable of and increased their financial wellbeing. They have formed new relationships with themselves and with others. Stress and overwhelm have taken a back seat, and confidence and clarity have taken centre stage.

Decision-making has become effortless, and almost everyone reports back that they feel more empowerment, more freedom, more peace and more joy in their lives, their work and their relationships.

INTRODUCTION

Changing yourself hasn't always seemed that simple to me, though. I remember thinking:

- You can't just reinvent yourself. What would people think?
- You can't be one person one day and then another the next.
- You can't suddenly have confidence. That wouldn't be authentic.

I had lots of ideas about who I was and who I wasn't, and I had lots of judgement on other people.

I didn't realise back then that those judgements of others were simply a reflection of the judgements I had on myself. Judgements that were keeping me stuck and playing small. Judgements that were coming from fear and insecurity. Judgements that did nothing to help free me, and everything to reinforce my stuckness and my 'shy girl' identity.

In 2018, I hired my first personal coach. While working with him, I discovered an understanding that changed my life. An understanding that I will share with you in this book.

That year marked the start of a paradigm shift for me. I left my corporate HR career and set up my own coaching business. I committed to living life on my terms, as the highest expression of myself. I learned to say no and set boundaries with grace and ease. I learned to listen to my intuition, to let go, to forgive, to trust in myself, to invest in myself, to ask for what I wanted, to own my value and my gifts.

I learned to care more about the things that matter and less about what others thought of me. More importantly, I learned to see through the illusion of what I thought of myself – an illusion that was limiting me in ways I hadn't even realised. Best of all, I came out from my hiding place and developed my voice. I now speak on podcasts and stages and have been honoured to be recognised by *USA TODAY* as an exceptional woman leader inspiring change.

In this book, I'll share some of the lessons I have learned – the real game changers that have created my new expansive life. I write from my heart to yours, to debunk the myths you may have innocently been programmed to believe about yourself and others – programming that puts limitations on what you believe you can achieve and impacts your entire experience of life.

My wish is that this book inspires you to:

- Let go of who you think you have to be

- Live from an understanding of who you truly are

Everyday people can do extraordinary things. Despite our best efforts, though, many of us struggle to understand this. We've heard people say *That's not for people like us,* and we've believed it.

Wouldn't it be great if we could rewire ourselves in a way that would propel us forward, in a way that would allow us to let go of the limiting ideas we've inherited? What if there was an understanding of the human design that allowed this process of letting go to be effortless? Well, there is – and I'm about to share it with you!

People come to me when they are ready to reimagine, redesign and reinvent their lives. When they want to get more comfortable within themselves. Or when they want to write the next chapter on their terms. My version of success won't be your version of success. Don't get wrapped up in my achievements, I want to know what *you* care about. This journey is about supporting you to live in alignment with *your* deeper calling. We'll be exploring what is true for *you*.

I don't know how much time we will all have in these human shells of ours, and I don't know why some of us get longer than others. However, I do believe that life is a precious gift. Mel Robbins shared in her TEDx Talk in San Francisco that scientists had calculated the odds of you being born, with your DNA structure and to your parents, as one in 400 trillion.[1] With that, I feel a delicious sense of obligation to make my time here count and to help others who want to, do the same.

I learned at a young age that I was shy, but I have now discovered my voice. I want my voice to have an impact and to be an inspiration, to pave the way for other voices to be seen and heard. To have people step into their greatness now – not later. I want to activate

---

1 M Robbins, 'How to stop screwing yourself over', TED Talk (June 2011), www.ted.com/talks/mel_robbins_how_to_stop_screwing_yourself_over, accessed 30 September 2024

the aliveness within so that people can make the most of the time they have remaining.

Ask yourself:

- What is the footprint you want to leave in the sand?

- What is the music inside you that wants to be expressed?

How we view ourselves is fundamental in enabling us to make our highest contribution. Don't reach the end of your time here with regrets. Don't die with your music inside you. Make the choice now to do something about this. Our lives are created and lived here, right now – the present moment is all we ever have.

I acknowledge you for being here with this book. The inner journey you are about to undertake is designed to disrupt self-limitations and make space for more expansive, invigorated and empowered being states to emerge. You will start to generate ideas about how you wish your life to be and about what is possible for you. You will start to navigate unknown and unfamiliar feelings. You will develop a deeper sense of self.

You will likely feel some resistance show up, as this book invites you to challenge your current understanding and beliefs – and the ego doesn't like to go down without a fight! You are not your ego, though. You are not the thoughts of your ego.

You are capable and whole, and you have an infinitely powerful ally to partner with in creating all of your heart's desires. In this book, I will introduce

INTRODUCTION

you to this ally. I will evoke in you a sense of possibility, freedom and expansiveness that will open up the doorway to the life you want to live, rather than your default future.

What if you are not who you have learned to believe you are?

How to get the most from this book

This book can be consumed in independent parts, thanks to its standalone sections and chapters; or if you prefer, you can read from cover to cover for a deeper, continuous journey. My recommendation is that you read from start to finish the first time and then come back to revisit the sections you are most drawn towards later.

Part One is all about understanding who we are and how we work, Part Two contains thirteen powerful life lessons to help you identify and shed unhelpful beliefs. Part Three will invite you to create your future life from a richer connection to your true self.

Activities are dotted throughout to help you bring the lessons in this book off the pages and into life. Don't skip them. They are there to help you embody what you are learning. Reading, alone, will give you an intellectual understanding; implementing what you learn will be your gateway to transformation.

I'll say this a different way because it is important and I am not here to be fluffy. You won't get what you want unless you put the work in.

It isn't enough to know about compound interest. The action of depositing the money is required for it to compound. We don't get what we want, we get who we're being, remember!

Throughout this book, I will share personal stories. While it can be tempting to read them thinking about the people concerned, I encourage you to listen to what is in each story for *you*. Be mindful of the message. Listen out for the principles that the stories convey rather than the context. For example, a story about personal relationships might wake you up to something playing out in business, and vice versa.

As you continue through this book, I encourage you to lean in and read with a curious, open mind. Many of us listen to what we're reading through our own already biased lens. We listen to agree or disagree; we listen to validate what we believe.

If 10,000 people read this book, there will be 10,000 versions of it because we are always listening to our mind's narrative about things. It would be the same content in all 10,000 copies, but there would be 10,000 different experiences. Which one is right? There is no *right*. There is simply thinking and believing there is.

As best you can, begin to notice how you're listening. I invite you to listen from a place within you that is open to possibility. To put aside, just for a little while, any strong opinions you might have and open yourself up to fresh insight. Open your mind and your heart, and listen from a place of curiosity and willingness to see something new. Give yourself the gift of being a beginner. You've nothing to prove here;

INTRODUCTION

no expert status is required. This kind of listening paves the way for insight and growth.

Isn't it peculiar that I just said *listen* to what you're reading? Unless you've got an audio version of the book, we don't usually talk about it this way. How can we listen to what we're reading? It's because we're listening to what we *think* about what we're reading. *We do that with all of life.*

As you go through the book, ask yourself: What are the insights and the lessons here for me? Where and how are they showing up in my life?

Ready? Let's create the new you.

PART ONE
A FRESH UNDERSTANDING

1
The Big Illusion

What if the things we have learned to believe make up our reality aren't quite accurate after all? What if the emotions we feel aren't triggered by what we think has caused them? What if our *reality* is an illusion created by the mind?

Have we been misled?

This chapter will show you how our thoughts and beliefs create our realities. If you can shift your relationship with your thoughts, you can transform your entire experience of life.

Advice for my younger self

People sometimes ask, 'What do you know now that you wish you knew back then?' What I am about to share with you would have to be up there in my top three answers. I truly wish this stuff was taught in schools. I think everyone – individuals, communities, organisations – would be far better off with this understanding. Here it is:

What you are experiencing is a result of your relationship to your thoughts. It is an inside job, and a whole new experience is available to you in any moment – regardless of circumstances.

Slow down. Read it again.

> What you are experiencing is a result of your relationship to your thoughts. It is an inside job, and a whole new experience is available to you in any moment – regardless of circumstances.

Let me bring this to life for you with my client Amanda.

CASE STUDY: Shifting perspectives

Amanda used to get annoyed about her partner leaving the dishes in the sink. She had a lot of thinking about this. Until I asked, 'If you got a call to say your partner had been in an accident and was in critical condition in hospital, what would happen to the thinking about the dishes in the sink?'

'Oh,' she said, and she dropped right out of her anger towards her partner. It happened in an instant.

The dishes were still in the sink, her partner hadn't been in an accident, and yet here she was having a completely different experience. The dishes seemed insignificant, and she was now experiencing guilt for thinking that way about her partner in the first place.

Isn't it fascinating how a change of thought can alter our whole experience of 'reality'? It's because it isn't exactly reality. It is an illusion we have been programmed to think and believe to be reality. We believe the thoughts that we are experiencing, and we develop strong attachments to our thoughts.

Where did Amanda's original thoughts about her partner go? How did her feelings of anger change to feelings of guilt?

The answer is that our thoughts and feelings can easily and instantly change or disappear when we learn not to get so involved with them. Our feelings are not facts – they are only a representation of our thinking. When we have angry thoughts, we experience the feeling of anger. When we have guilty thoughts, we experience the sensation of guilt. We experience our thoughts all day long, yet we don't stop to consider that this is what is happening – that our thoughts are creating our emotional state.

Instead, we attribute our feelings to something that has happened outside of us – a circumstance, a person, an event. We think that thing outside of us is what caused our feelings. It looks that way, right? We notice the correlation – the person did leave the dishes in the sink and then I got mad. If he hadn't left the dishes in the sink, I wouldn't be mad about it. What we have missed noticing is that the thoughts about the dishes being in the sink are what created the feeling – not the person, not the dishes, not the sink. At any moment we can experience a new thought but not if we get attached to the old one.

Our thoughts are at the heart of what drives our behaviour. Our thoughts impact how we interact with others, with ourselves, and with our environments. They impact our financial health, our careers, our relationships and our wellbeing.

> Our automatic, daily behaviour is a reaction to unquestioned thoughts and feelings.

Amanda believes her partner should not leave the dishes in the sink and that it means he doesn't respect her. The dishes are in the sink – that is reality. The idea that this means he doesn't respect Amanda is not reality. It is an opinion. It is Amanda's *truth*, but it is not absolute truth. It is not truth with a capital T. In that moment, though, Amanda really believes that she is right. She has lost sight of it being a thought and believes it to be truth with a capital T. From there, she behaves a certain way with her partner, which creates a breakdown in their relationship and they decide to separate. Her reality is now that she has no partner.

Believing our thinking is what creates our *perception of reality*, and it drives our behaviour. Our behaviour is what creates tangible results. Some results we want and others we do not!

According to research from Queen's University in Canada, the average person has around 6,200 'thought worms' per day.[2] (Thought worms are a chain of consecutive thoughts about a specific topic.[3]) That's a lot of thoughts moving through us!

If we are consciously and unconsciously reacting to our thoughts all day long, surely then it makes sense to give this topic some airtime.

Let's take a deeper look at this big driver of our lives.

The nature of thought – the simplest route to peace and happiness

When I first heard people talk about the nature of thought, I struggled to get my head around what they meant. Nature of thought? *Nature* of thought?

---

2   A Craig, 'Discovery of "thought worms" opens window to the mind', *Queen's University Gazette* (13 July 2020), www.queensu.ca/gazette/stories/discovery-thought-worms-opens-window-mind, accessed 1 October 2024
3   Ibid.

I didn't understand the question, let alone why it even mattered! And yet here I am, all these years later, talking about the same thing with amplified excitement. Now I've realised that this understanding is the simplest, most direct route to a happier, more peaceful and expansive life – and there is less to *do* than we think.

When I reference the nature of thought, in the simplest terms, it's all about the following questions:

- What is thought made of?
- Where does it come from?
- Where does it go?
- What do I mean about us experiencing our thoughts?

Thought is a neutral, ever-changing and formless energy. It isn't something we can see or touch or hold; it is an energy that moves through us – transient, invisible energy. Thoughts naturally arise and pass through our minds, back into the formless universal energy from which they came. Like a wave in the ocean, it has its moment as a unique, individual wave, and then it goes back into the vastness of the ocean.

There's a popular metaphor in my profession used to highlight the nature of thought and our innate wellbeing.

The nature of thought

Take a look at the clouds in the sky. Notice how they are always moving. Some look fluffy and white; some look dark and stormy. At times they mask the sun. Then, without us needing to do anything, they move on by, and the sun reveals itself again to us. That is the nature of clouds – transient energy. Clouds are like thoughts that way.

The sun represents our innate wellbeing. Ever present. Always available. Always there, but the clouds – our thoughts – sometimes conceal it. We don't need to worry about moving the clouds along or worrying if the sun is there because we know that is naturally happening. It just is.

We don't seem to understand that with our thoughts, however. Especially the dark and stormy ones. We tend to worry about them and want to move them along. Guess what worry is, though – more dark and stormy thoughts! Instead of moving the thoughts along, we're adding more to the mix.

Why do we do that? Why do we get so involved with our thoughts at times?

It is because we think nothing will change if we don't get involved. We get so preoccupied with the *content* of them, that we forget about their *nature*. Not realising that if we didn't get so attached to them, they would move along all by themselves. Making space for more helpful thoughts to come along.

The ironic thing is that we naturally leave a lot of our thoughts alone all day long. We have many thoughts that we don't get invested in – that we don't even really notice. They come and go. *Hi, peek-a-boo. Hello… Nope, didn't even notice… Gone…* next! Have you ever gone in to a room and forgotten what you went in there for? Perhaps you wanted to say something and, in the next moment, your mind goes blank and you can't remember what you wanted to say. Where did those thoughts go?

Next time you're experiencing a stormy thought, have the clouds remind you that this thought shall pass. Simply notice what happens when you allow it to be there, without judgement or resistance. It is the resistance which causes it to linger, and the judgement that invites its friends to join in.

I promise that when you drop out of the thinking that is taking you away from peace, you'll fall back into a nicer feeling and more clarity of mind. From that space within, higher-quality ideas will sprout.

Here are some common thoughts that we experience in our lives. Do any of these sound familiar to you?

- She/he/they should know better.
- What if it goes wrong?
- That is so embarrassing.
- My boss doesn't like me.
- Why did I say I would do that?
- What if I never meet anyone?
- No one listens to me.
- What are they saying about me?
- What if I don't succeed?
- I'm not a good enough friend/daughter/son/parent/sibling/partner.
- I'm not smart enough.
- I'll never be able to do that.
- Money is for other people.
- Success is for other people.
- It will take too long.
- It will be too difficult.
- I'll never find love.

- I'm not seen.
- I'm not appreciated.
- I'm not consistent.
- I'll do it tomorrow.
- They are waiting for me to fail.
- I ignore red flags.
- Vulnerability is weakness.
- Self-love is egotistical.
- Who I am to have that?
- If I aspire for more, I will end up disappointed.
- I don't have time.
- There must be something wrong with me.
- I can't ask for help.
- I'm not worthy.
- I can't afford it.
- I shouldn't have said or done that.
- I shouldn't be angry.
- I'm too old.
- I'm too young.
- I'm not going to ever achieve my potential.
- I'm too insecure.

- I'm out of control.
- I have trust issues.
- People will laugh at me.

Do any of these sound familiar? Now we're coming to the end of the first chapter, I invite you to spend time with an activity. As I mentioned in the introduction, each one has been designed to help you fully receive the gifts within these pages, so allow yourself the space and time to dive in.

Choose your preferred way of taking notes. I recommend you keep all your notes from these activities together so you can easily reflect on them and add new insights over time.

I have also created a free downloadable collection of all the activities in this book, together with relevant headings, structure and space for your reflections, which you may find helpful. To access the collection go to https://trulyyoubook.com/resources.

ACTIVITY: Noticing thoughts

Take a moment to write down the thoughts you experience regularly. Maybe they are similar to the ones listed here. Maybe not. Either way is great. This is going to be your journey, and there is no right or wrong. At this stage, you're simply growing in awareness of the thoughts you experience. You don't need to change or fix anything.

Read the lines below, taking each area of life one at a time and then list the thoughts that come to you.

When I think about work/relationships/family/money/friends, the thoughts I experience more regularly are...

As you write the thoughts down, see if you can bring a sense of compassion to the process. Then take a moment to simply be with them. Breathe and notice. Let yourself reflect and observe from love, compassion and curiosity, these thoughts running through your mind.

You don't have to complete all the categories in one go. Choose where you are most pulled to explore and come back to the others another time. Which of the areas do you want to prioritise? Work? Family?

As you go about your day, start to notice the thoughts you are experiencing and where you feel the sensations stimulated by those thoughts in your body. You might even notice the sensation *before* you are aware of the thought. That's the body's way of waking us up to our thinking.

Come back to the activity and write your reflections down. What patterns or themes do you spot in your thinking? Do they focus on fears, judgements or hopes? Just notice.

Key insights

- Our personal realities are created through how we interpret our thoughts and how we relate to that interpretation.

- That interpretation then influences our behaviour, and that behaviour shapes the tangible results we see (and don't see) in our lives.

- Feelings are not facts; instead, they are a reflection of our thinking in the moment.

- Thoughts are like passing clouds, transient, formless energy that is ever changing. Like clouds, thoughts pass without our interference. Our innate wellbeing is always present.

- Detaching ourselves from our thought creates space for new, fresh thinking to emerge.

- You are only ever one thought away from a new experience.

2
It's An Inside Job

In this chapter, we explore the role our feelings play in measuring our clarity of mind in each moment. We uncover an approach to life that invites freedom from within so that we're not left battling against our circumstances in search of peace and wellbeing. Plus, we learn how to take the personal out of any experience so that we can see more clearly the truth of who we are.

First though, let's start with a really important point, because if you've created your list of thoughts (from Chapter One's activity), and you notice they are a little on the critical side, then I could be painting a picture of thought being the bad guy here. If that is happening, I want to get in there and correct the course. I don't want to demonise thought. Thought is neutral. I know I called some of our thoughts dark and stormy earlier – but without a judgement on the labels *dark* and *stormy*, these thoughts are all neutral.

It's what we *do* with our thoughts that starts to create problems for us. How we *relate* to our thinking is what gets us stuck. Problems come from the meaning we apply, and humans are meaning-making machines. Luckily for us, this is great news because it is news we can use! Letting go of that meaning is how we can start to get unstuck. We simply need to wake up to the fact that we are applying meaning. More good news to come because we have a built-in alarm clock for that – our feelings.

The heart's barometer

Many of my mentors, teachers and guides have pointed me to this: that our thoughts create our feelings.

> We are only ever feeling our thoughts; we are not directly feeling our circumstances.

This was wildly different to anything I had heard before and wildly different to how I thought life worked. To begin with, I had a lot of resistance to what my mentors were suggesting. I thought my circumstances were to blame for my feelings. Although I also had a lot of curiosity around this and I was hungry to understand more.

I remember observing my mentors and thinking they looked like they knew the secret to life. There was a sparkle in their eyes and a glow about them. It seemed like they loved life. I wanted to believe what they were saying because there was something they seemed to know here, that I hadn't yet grasped. And I wanted more sparkle and glow!

The also said to me:

Your feelings are a barometer of your clarity of thought in any particular moment in time.

The more intense the feeling, the more likely our thinking is off track, yet the more intense the feeling, the more we tend to believe our thinking. When we're experiencing intense feelings such as embarrassment, anger, fear or worry, we're likely not even aware that the feeling is being generated by some thinking that we're treating as truth with a capital T.

Feelings barometer

We tend to look for the escape route out of the feeling of discomfort we are in. And this is the cool thing: we mistakenly believe that the feeling of discomfort has come from something outside of us. We therefore look to change our circumstances rather than looking at the real cause of the feelings – the story running in our mind's eye and the meaning we are placing on our circumstances.

Why would we look to the story – the meaning, if we think it is a circumstance, event or person that has created the feeling? Why would we know to do this, if no one has taught us this before?

The result of this misunderstanding is that we're running around putting sticky plasters on the wound (changing the circumstances, which often includes trying to change another person), but we're not addressing the source of the wound (believing our thinking). We might be thinking things like:

- I didn't like his attitude.
- They need to be more considerate.
- She needs to stop doing that.

Suddenly, we've put our Captain Superiority pants on and think everyone should do as we would do because we know best.

This way of being is a fast track to exhaustion, relationship breakdowns and unhappiness. Other people don't tend to love it when we tell them what is wrong with them and try to get them to change in a way that suits our view of the world. Would you?

The next time you feel a burning desire to tell someone how they need to change, pause. Experiment with not trusting your thinking in that moment. What if you are not experiencing clarity? What if you are experiencing and believing low-grade thinking, which is way off track from the Truth? What if that intense feeling is actually your body's alarm clock saying *don't trust your thinking right now*?

How's that for a different way of looking out at the world?

How might that impact your relationships for the better when you're not reacting to a story full of judgements and assumptions that are causing a feeling of anger?

How might that have you be *more* impactful, not less when you're not communicating from a story full of judgements and assumptions that are causing a feeling of frustration or righteousness?

So what exactly is going on? Let's look at the brilliant wisdom of inside-out living.

Outside-in vs inside-out living

Most people believe that our happiness and our pain come from the *outside-in*. We think that someone else is the problem, that our circumstances are creating our feelings, that it's all out there. We need a different partner, a new job, more money. We need that person to stop making us feel this way. When this or that changes, we can be happy.

Boy, it is exhausting, thinking we need to change all this. Equally, it is exhausting having to live up to other people's expectations. It is exhausting having a heart at war in this way. We don't realise that our whole experience of life is created from the *inside-out*, from how we think about what is happening. The creation comes from within us, from within our mind, but we are not aware of that.

You are always only one thought away from a different reality.

We have been given the most incredible gift of thought, and yet so often, we turn it against ourselves and others. We use it to create limits in our mind about who we are and what we're capable of, and to cast judgements that separate us from each other.

What if instead, we chose to use this inside-out living in more helpful ways? To cultivate more empowered states of mind. More resourceful, creative thinking. To see the good in an experience, in a person, in ourselves. What if we cultivated that kind of programming instead of the current automated unhelpful thought loops that are on repeat? We'll talk more about how to cultivate this later in the book. For now, I want to introduce you to the voice of the ego mind because this trickster right here is the one setting off the alarm and then denying all knowledge.

The voice of the ego mind

You might know this voice as the inner critic, the saboteur, the chimp on the shoulder. It might express itself as righteousness, blame or sarcasm. The list goes on because the ego mind wears *a lot* of disguises.

Like a world-class marketing expert, it will convince you of anything and then say, *'It wasn't me!'* With practice and intention, it is possible to develop a new relationship with the voice of the ego mind – a relationship that will invite you to witness its voice without letting it define you, a relationship that will serve your highest good and nurture your growth. Believe it or not, we can actually use the voice of the ego mind to identify parts of ourselves that are craving some love and attention. It can help us to see ourselves on a deeper level. Most of us don't get to understand that, though, as we try to push it away, ignore it and resist it. I'm going to help you develop a different relationship with the voice of the ego mind throughout this book.

Now, you won't find an ego inside you because it isn't something tangible we can identify in the brain like the hippocampus or the amygdala. However, we all get lured in by this intangible energy regularly. If you think that doesn't apply to you, my friend, *that* is the voice of the ego!

Dictionaries define the ego as your sense of self-esteem, your opinion of yourself or your self-image. I like to describe the ego as the collection of unquestioned thoughts and beliefs. It is the 'I' that we often identify with. It is the talkative personal mind that constantly judges and compares, and which cares more about feeling right and looking good than seeking truth.

You might notice its presence in your list of thoughts from the activity in Chapter One. As we let go of our attachment to its stories, it lets go of us. From there, wisdom can take the remote control.

The operating system

Let's look in more detail at the human design. I'm illustrating for you what I like to call the *operating system* and it is at the heart of everything I share in this book.

It highlights that:

- Our thoughts create our feelings
- Our feelings drive our behaviours
- Our behaviours shape our results

Thought → Feelings → Behaviours → Results

The operating system

Imagine a computer that is spouting out an error message. To fix the error, you don't change the screen, the keyboard or the computer itself. You go to the heart of the issue – the data – and you change the input.

You can't put sausages on a BBQ and expect to get a burger on your plate. Put sausages on the BBQ and you will get sausages on your plate. Want a burger? Change the input!

You can't have shitty thoughts about your partner and expect to feel intimacy and a deep sense of love and connection. Want love and connection? Change the input!

> You put garbage in, you'll get garbage out. Do you want a different result? Change the input.

Now, this might have sounded simple until I threw in the partner example, right? That's because we get so attached to our thoughts. We treat them as facts, and the ego finds all the evidence it can to support its way of thinking:

- My partner *doesn't* listen to me.
- He *does* flirt with other women.
- He *is* always leaving his dirty socks *next* to the laundry basket.

The ego doesn't want to change the data. The ego wants to be right.

Those statements might be true. Your partner might always leave his socks next to the laundry basket – I'm not saying that is an illusion. I'm saying that we create our personal experience of that situation using our minds. Notice how multiple thoughts flood your mind when you spot mislaid socks for the umpteenth time. Thoughts are what put the meaning on things and what intensifies the feeling you're experiencing.

He left his socks next to the laundry basket is neutral. That is, until we add:

- That means he disrespects me.
- That means he doesn't care.
- He treats me like his maid.
- Does he think I haven't got anything better to do than tidy up after him?

Now all of a sudden we're lost in a thought storm and can say bye-bye to intimacy and connection!

Sometimes our thoughts even convince us that this thought storm moment is the *perfect* moment to tell him who he is and how he uses us too. It is also the perfect moment to add in how he looked at that woman in the restaurant the other night, and how he never sticks up for you with your mother-in-law. Can you see how, when we're in the thick of the thought storm and the feeling is getting more intense, we get more and more lost in our story of our partner, all of which was triggered by our thoughts about his sock habit?

This is what I mean when I say our feelings are the barometer for the clarity of our thought right now. The more intense the feeling, the more important it is to take a pause and then take another look. If you're going for connection and intimacy, you're not going to get there from a heart at war.

A thought storm

Don't worry – this is most definitely not a book about tolerating poor behaviour or about being a doormat. Hell, no – this is about empowerment and freedom and joy. It is about creating a full and expansive life from a place of love and clarity of mind. If you're thinking that the alternative option to making your partner the problem is to be pushed around or spend a lifetime picking up their socks, please think again. That is not the alternative option that I see. We'll go into more detail about this in Lesson 12, 'Allow Everything, Accommodate Little'.

You might by now have noticed some resistance to what you have been reading, and you might have a lot of questions, just like I did when I was introduced to the inside-out understanding. This is great because I don't want you to take my word for it. I want you to try it out and see something for yourself. This is the difference between an intellectual understanding and an embodied understanding. It is the difference between someone describing to you what an orgasm is like and you having one for the first time – totally different, right?

For now, I encourage you to practise noticing the thoughts you are having throughout the day. Observe yourself, and observe your mind's narrative. Awareness is the first step in transformation. I call this, *witness consciousness*, and this is what allows us to get some distance from thought so that we can take a more objective look.

Witness consciousness

Imagine your mind is a busy train station with trains on different tracks moving in and out of the station all day long.

The trains represent your different thoughts, feelings and beliefs. Most of the time we are so caught up in catching the train that we don't even notice the platform. We're too busy jumping on one thought, riding it for a while then jumping on to the next.

Witness consciousness is like stepping back onto the platform instead of riding the train. It's about trainspotting without feeling the need to get on board. You are the quiet, still presence of the platform, simply observing all the movement of the trains.

With witness consciousness, you see that you are the one who *notices* thoughts. You see that you are the platform, not the trains.

The witness is a deeper aspect of your consciousness. It can step back and observe the mind's activity.

Witness consciousness allows us to get some distance from our thoughts and freedom to see more clearly. When that distance is not there, thoughts become personal – and when that happens we will defend them to the hills. Take a look at what happens in meetings; people are so proud of their ideas, fixed in their ways, defensive of their suggestions and afraid to disagree with someone's solution for fear of offending. We take our thoughts personally all the time, and the quality of our listening as a result takes a severe nose dive.

By separating our thoughts from our identity, we release the emotional charge they carry and stay present and open. We're able to respond from clarity and grounding rather than reacting impulsively. How differently might you respond if you saw someone was attacking *a* thought, not attacking *my* idea? The thought isn't you. You are simply the vessel it chose to land in, and from which it is being expressed.

Key insights

- Thoughts are neutral – they are not the bad guy. What we do with our thoughts can make us feel stuck or unstuck.

- The more we identify with our thoughts, the more intense the feeling we experience. An intense feeling is not an indicator of Truth.

- Feelings are the heart's barometer – they are a guide to the clarity of mind you are in at any one moment.

- Freedom comes from within, not from our circumstances. An inside-out approach to life shows that our thinking about our circumstances is what creates our experience of them.

- The ego mind has many disguises and is constantly adding meaning and judgement to situations.

- You are not your ego, neither is the ego an enemy. The ego is simply a misguided friend with unquestioned thoughts and beliefs who can help wake us up to parts of ourselves that require love.

- The operating system: our thoughts create our feelings, which drive our behaviours and determine our results. If we want different results, we must relate to our thinking differently.

- Witness consciousness allows us to detach from thought and observe them like trains in a station. This perspective reduces reactivity and removes the personal from them.

3
Thought Is A Superpower

In the last two chapters, I have emphasised the importance of detaching ourselves from unhelpful thoughts, not making them our identity and instead simply observing our thoughts as they come and go. This chapter will remind us of how important and helpful our thoughts can be too. Even the 'unhelpful' ones. Yes, I know that sounds like an oxymoron. How can something unhelpful also be helpful? Don't worry – we will get to all of that.

In this next part, I am going to use labels such as *positive* and *negative* for ease of communicating; however, technically, all thought is neutral. We're the ones who assign judgements like helpful and unhelpful. We can choose to use thought to limit us or we can choose to use thought to empower us. We have an active role to play here.

A client once asked me a powerful question as we were exploring some of her limiting beliefs. 'If these negative thoughts aren't true, then aren't the positive ones made up also? Aren't they all just constructs?' She was touching on a great point. Whether we find comfort or challenge, a thought is a passing experience within us – and we get to decide what role each thought plays in our life. I smiled and replied 'Absolutely! Wouldn't you rather spend time with the ones that bring out your greatness?'

Imagine thought being like a garden: it can grow weeds or flowers depending on the seeds you plant and the care you give it.

Thought is not the enemy

Our brains are wired to avoid risk and keep us safe, so it makes sense that we have a lot of fearful limiting thoughts that enter our minds. Here's the important point, though, *we can override the wiring.*

When I work with people on thought and their belief systems, they learn how thought creates their personal realities. They understand that we experience our circumstances through our thinking about those circumstances. They understand that we experience ourselves through our thinking about ourselves. That includes negative thoughts such as:

- I am not confident.
- I didn't do a great job on that last presentation.

THOUGHT IS A SUPERPOWER

- Mrs Whatsherface at work is constantly criticising me; she's out to get me.

These thoughts create unwanted feelings and limitations in their lives. The next questions then become:

- How do I stop thinking?
- How do I get rid of these thoughts? Because they're spoiling my fun over here.

I say, 'Whoa – steady on there, my friend. The ability to think is a gift – a wild and precious gift! Thought is how we experience life. Imagine having no thought. You'd be brain-dead. That doesn't sound like the option I would choose. How about we meet somewhere else? Let's start to look at thought as a *superpower.'*

If you can use thought to beat yourself up and tell yourself you're not good enough, then what if you could use thought to do the opposite? What if you could use your imagination to serve you? To bring you ideas? To dream bigger and live more expansively? What if you could use thought to have you see your brilliance and your gifts? How great does all that sound?

Take a look around you. What do you see? As I'm typing this on my MacBook, I am grateful for the thoughts of the people who wondered if we could create electricity, keyboards, laptops, word processors and printers. Gosh, imagine if those people had no thoughts – none of this would have come to form.

Who had the idea to create books? To create libraries? To create publishing businesses?

Everything around us is created from ideas brought to life. What are ideas? Thought. What is imagination? Thought. Those people I see living their most authentic, aligned lives are those who are using thought to serve them, to find reasons to bring their creations to life. Those who use thought to find reasons to limit themselves and hold themselves back are misunderstanding and misusing this miraculous capacity we have to think. Thought is a wonderful gift that we have been blessed with. Use your gift – your superpower – wisely!

CASE STUDY: The impact of what we listen to

In his book, *The Hidden Messages in Water*, Japanese scientist Dr Masaru Emoto found that when exposed to words and music during the freezing process, water crystallised in different ways.

The water exposed to uplifting music, and to words such as *love* and *gratitude*, formed into beautiful and symmetrical crystals. Meanwhile, the water exposed to heavy metal music and words such as *You disgust me* formed disconnected and disfigured crystals.

While critics argue that his work lacks rigorous scientific controls, the research has inspired others to explore the potential connection between consciousness and the physical environment.

Your unique curriculum

In the same way you are experiencing a unique set of thoughts, you are also experiencing your unique curriculum. By curriculum, I mean life and all its surprises – the highs, the lows and everything in between. This curriculum can't be fully known in advance, which can be difficult for us humans because we are often so uncomfortable with the unknown. We crave control over our lives, but life has a lot of uncertainty – that is a given. If those unknowns are going to exist anyway, even without our blessing, wouldn't it be better to embrace them? I think so, there is more peace and freedom to be found this way.

Throughout our lives, we're taught that knowing is important. We get praise for correct answers in an exam. We get recognised at work for being an expert in our field. We want to know more information so we can make informed choices.

Conversely, we may have been laughed at, called names or rejected when we didn't know things. The subconscious notices how unsafe it felt in those moments, and lodges a note internally to avoid that in the future. This can make us believe that knowing is good, and not knowing – or admitting we don't know – is bad. We're conditioned to believe that the more we know, the safer we will be.

It is no surprise then that we might struggle with the unknown. Knowing gives us a sense of control and safety. If there are no guarantees in life, though, and we're not in control of everything, why on earth are we placing our peace and wellbeing on knowing?

Is there a way to be more comfortable with the unknown?

Yes, there is!

Embracing the mystery of the unknown

Instead of worrying about not being able to control everything around us, what if we embraced the perspective that all of life was showing up to help us, regardless of whether we liked it or not? What if everything around us was here to serve our evolution? What if the unique set of circumstances, events and people that we encounter in our lifetime becomes our unique curriculum to work with so that we can grow here in earth school?

I don't know the reasons behind why a lot of things happen. I don't know why some people are taken from us earlier than others, why some get sick and others don't, why some find love and others don't. (Sorry, Simon Sinek – I'm a big fan of *Start With Why*, but sometimes the why is beyond the understanding of the logical mind.[4])

In life, there is always the reality of any situation. I call this 'What is'. Then there is what we think should be happening in that situation. I call this 'Preference'.

---

4   S Sinek, *Start With Why: How great leaders inspire everyone to take action* (Portfolio, 2009)

For example, 'What is': *I don't know what is about to happen.* Preference: *I need to know what is about to happen.* The gap between these two points is what causes our suffering.

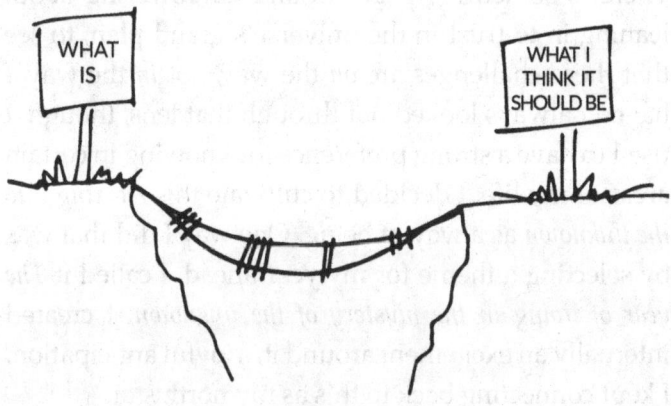

The suffering gap

In Steve Jobs' famous Stanford speech, he pointed to how life is unpredictable and that we can't always see how things are coming together.[5] He said that means you can only connect the dots looking backwards. When he dropped out of college and took up a 'random' calligraphy class, he had no idea that this class would influence the design of the Mac computer years later, making it the first to feature beautiful typography. What seems like a random choice or a wrong path might well lead to something more

---

5   S Jobs, 'Steve Jobs to 2005 graduates: "Stay hungry, stay foolish"', *Stanford Report* (12 June 2005), https://news.stanford.edu/news/2005/june15/jobs-061505.html, accessed 2 October 2024

beautiful than you could ever imagine from your 'knowing' of the personal intellect.

I like to trust that something greater than my intelligence is at play, and that it knows better than me. There is something peaceful and empowering about leaning in to trust in the universe's grand plan, to see that these challenges are *on* the way, not *in* the way. I haven't always looked out through that lens, though. I used to have a strong preference for knowing in certain areas of my life. I decided to cultivate this *relaxing into the unknown* as a way of being. One way I did that was by selecting a theme for my year ahead. I called it *The year of living in the mystery of the unknown*. I created internally an excitement around it, a joyful anticipation. I kept connecting back to this as my north star.

To relate to it this way is a choice – a choice of attitude. This choice is yours to make too. I'm not here to tell you what to believe or what to choose. I am here to be a stand for your freedom and empowerment – and for that to happen now, not later. My *north star* commitment is an example of how we can live our learnings. It is an example of how we get who we're being. I am much more at peace and excited with the unknown these days – and I have made bolder life choices from the freedom I have found around this.

All of life is my teacher and is showing up to help me realise who I truly am.

THOUGHT IS A SUPERPOWER

If trusting in the natural unfolding of life is something you find a challenge, start by exploring where the wisdom of it has already played out in your life. Take a moment to look back on times that felt unclear or difficult and notice the gifts and growth that have come from them. What dots can you now join?

ACTIVITY: Recognising gain and growth

Grab your notebook and write down points on the following. Structure your notes in a list with three columns with the headings: **What didn't make sense at the time**, **gain or growth**, and **larger plan**.

1. Take a look back through your life and note down one or two experiences or events that felt challenging, unclear or confusing at the time. Write these in the first column.
2. In the second column, for each experience, explore how you grew as a result and/or what you gained from that time in your life. Think about the skills learned, strengths you developed and perspectives that emerged.
3. Consider how the experience might have been part of a larger plan. What was it getting you ready for? Jot this in the third column. It is OK if your answer to the third point is unknown as yet. Maybe that answer is still to be revealed.

Let the answers come to you – there's no need to force this. Stay open-minded, and the answers might well come when you least expect them.

Our growth areas

This might seem like a strange invitation, but I invite you to try out being OK with the things that go against your preferences.

- I am feeling anxious, and that's OK.
- My relationship ended, and that's OK.
- I snapped at my son, and that's OK.
- Life feels hard, and that's OK.

Let go of any judgement on things being hard. Let go of any judgement on the ego when it adds more layers of thought. If we don't make hard a problem, if we don't make layers a problem, if we don't make ego a problem, we automatically move closer to being accepting of what is, and away from being in resistance to it. Guess what happens when you drop the resistance. You move out of the suffering gap, you drop into a nicer feeling and you make space in your mind for higher-quality thinking to come through.

You might even feel some resistance to dropping the resistance. I know I have felt that many times in my life. Why? Because we mistakenly believe that if we let go of the resistance nothing will change. It doesn't mean that. I am not asking you to be passive or give up your agency to create. Surrendering the resistance is simply like clearing out the cupboard of rubbish so you have space for more quality items. Resistance and judgement take up so much bandwidth in our minds.

Letting them go creates some internal freedom to think differently.

As we navigate the growth offered by our life's curriculum, there are two powerful perspectives here for you to consider.

1. Internal transformation

Even more valuable than reaching the moon is the internal transformation that occurs in a person shooting for the moon. What do I mean by that? Who we become in the process is more valuable than any accomplishment of the material goal. That internal transformation is a huge gift, regardless of how the circumstances turn out.

- I *get* to handle a difficult client, in service of my growth as a leader.

- I *get* to experience grief, in service of a deeper compassion and patience with and for others.

- I *get* to go through heartbreak, in service of breaking free from the idea that I can't handle hurt and pain, or to see that heartbreak is beautiful as it shows me my infinite capacity to love.

Are you the leader, business owner, partner or friend you are today as a result of some of the difficult times you have experienced, or as a result of some of those things you believed at the time were *in* the way, not *on* the way?

Our curriculum is here to amplify life, so that each experience can be felt more fully, more freely and more richly, to expand us and to expand what we are capable of. What if everything is happening to show us our true selves? To bring out more of our gifts, not less. To help us stretch into the beings that we truly are. To ensure we don't short-change ourselves due to a misunderstanding of who we think we are.

This richness of life is available to everyone. We all have the capacity for this. We can all choose to use our curriculum in this way, to evolve our souls. If all of life was effortless, we wouldn't grow. Imagine a life where you were grateful for each experience. Where you embraced and used the full tour, not just the highlights. What if the next challenge you face is not something to be bypassed? What if it is getting you ready for your next-level success?

2. Writing the next chapter

This second powerful perspective is that *each new moment is full of potential*. We get to pick up the pen and write the next chapter, yet we can forget that when something we didn't want to have happen came true. We stop writing and ruminate there.

One of my favourite questions to ask myself and my clients is, 'Given what you have shared, what would you love to create now?'

'*I snapped at my son, and that's OK*' might then become... '*I'd love to create a heartfelt apology and have him know I love him more than anything.'* Or *'I'd love to heal the part of me that believes his behaviours represent my worthiness.'*

People forget about the creation part. When we're ruminating on what we didn't want, we are disconnected from our inner power to create a different outcome. We have lost connection to our higher self, to that part of us that already knows what to do, to the sun behind the clouds.

I used to have an illogical fear of being made homeless. I don't think it is a coincidence that I have been paired up with two incredible women in my lifetime in different coaching programmes who have both been homeless and who are now millionaires.

Fear can make us believe that the outcomes we dread are permanent. That we have no agency to create change, to be the author of our future. I can see now how much of an illusion that is.

I remember a mentor saying to me once, 'Lisa, if you ended up on the street, you would be the bag lady that taught all the other bag ladies how to get themselves off the street!'

Writing the next chapter in our life isn't about denying the circumstances we are in. It is about seeing that we don't have to let them define our future. Just like our past doesn't define our future, our current circumstances don't have to either. We can wake up to that at any moment.

I'm also sensitive to the fact that some circumstances *are* beyond our control when the outcome really is the final outcome, such as death and dying. When we can't change the circumstances, the power lies in changing your relationship with your thinking about the circumstances. We don't have to deny our pain, our grief, our loss. We don't have to deny our circumstances. When we allow the emotion to be there, when we don't resist it, when we surrender to it – that alone can move us into a deeper peace within.

We humans have the gift of free will, and we can use that gift to choose how we relate to our circumstances and our unique curriculums. That's where the agency lies in those types of circumstances so that we can have a different experience of them. I'm not saying it is easy, and it doesn't have to be. We humans can also do hard things.

In March 2022, I was at an event with Byron Katie for nine days. She was recalling a story from a time in her life when she thought she was going to meet her maker. Instead of relaying details of panic and worry, she told us what she had been thinking in that moment: 'If this is my last breath on earth, I don't want to miss the trip.' I heard that as the most powerful invitation into presence, regardless of what is happening around us. What a commitment to living and experiencing every moment in full bloom.

> **ACTIVITY: Exploring current challenges**
>
> In your notebook, write down the answers to the following questions:
>
> - What are you finding challenging right now?
> - How might it be showing up *for* you?
> - Why would you look forward to it happening again?

Key insights

- Thought is a superpower – an incredible gift that we can use to empower us or limit us. As in a garden, we can choose to grow flowers or weeds.

- Those who are living the most aligned, authentic lives are using their gift of thought wisely.

- Our unique curriculums are here to serve our own growth and evolution. They cannot be known in advance. The dots can only be joined by looking back.

- As we learn to embrace the unknown as an opportunity to grow, we can create a healthier relationship with uncertainty and put our trust in life's unfolding.

- We find ourselves suffering when we resist what is, in favour of our preference for what we think should be. Accepting what is opens us up to a more peaceful feeling.

- Surrendering resistance doesn't mean things can't change – instead, it expands the mind's bandwidth to receive fresh ideas.

- Each new moment is full of potential. Choose to create, not ruminate. Focus on what you can create next instead of fixating on what hasn't gone as you had planned.

- We always have a choice. We have free will to choose how we relate to our circumstances. Even when we cannot change the circumstances themselves, we can change our experience of them from the inside-out.

4
Your Powerful Ally

As nice and as simple as it sounds, to just accept my curriculum and trust that what is happening is here *for* me, I found it tricky to surrender to the unknown. To get out of the universe's way. I felt I had to learn how to do that. I had a lot of things that I cared about, and I didn't want to give up on them. How exactly could I do this surrendering without becoming passive? I'm about to share my experience with you.

Black dot vs white space

My mentors were adamant that I was already surrendering my thoughts many times a day. I found that hard to believe, though. It didn't feel safe to let go of the *important ones*. It felt like moving into acceptance meant that nothing would change. It felt like rolling over, giving in and/or giving up. It felt passive and I had work to do.

I protested (in a whiny voice), 'But we don't live in an equal world. The justice system is broken, people are still dying of hunger, homelessness is rife. Bullies are in leadership roles. We can't just flipping find peace with all this and say *Oh well, that's that, then!*'

Not put off by me, one of my wonderful mentors, Dicken Bettinger, pointed me to a different way with a simple picture:

Black dot on white paper

The expansive space around the dot is the infinite intelligence of the universe. The dot represents the intelligence of the personal mind.

When Dicken was sharing the picture with me, I was super-focused. I was listening and excited about what he was going to tell me. I was thinking, *Excellent – I'm this dot. Got it! I'm going to listen so well and then, in just a moment, when I have this new wisdom you are giving me, I will be able to use my dot so well to make the world a better place. Show me how, Dicken!*

He was not showing me how to use my dot better. (*Damn it – fooled again!*) Dicken was showing me what else was available. He was introducing me to the ally I promised you earlier in this book.

Dicken wasn't saying I needed to surrender to the fact we can't create a better world. He was saying that I had a more powerful force to create from than I realised. He was saying, 'Stop working the dot so hard and you will have *more* impact, not less.'

Learning to surrender

When we stop focusing on the dot, we can allow an infinite intelligence to move through us. When we get the personal mind out of the way, we open up the doorway to access a deeper wisdom. The white space is the master; the dot is the servant. I had been trying to create only from the dot. I'd had my operating manual the wrong way round.

Just like Steve Jobs in his Stanford speech, Dicken was saying that the personal mind – the dot – can't know what is for the best because it sees only a tiny fraction of the bigger plan. It likes to think it knows it all, but in reality, the dot's intellect is full of assumptions. It is also blind and ignorant to the fact that it is full of assumptions. The following case study illustrates the interaction between my dot and the white space.

CASE STUDY: My health scare

In 2022 I felt some bruising on my chest. I decided to make a doctor's appointment to get checked out.

The doctor didn't find any lump, but she referred me to the hospital for a mammogram, just to be on the safe side. My mind kept telling me to cancel the appointment, *There's no lump, you're totally fine. Give the space up to someone who needs it.* Yet, something made me keep the appointment.

I had the mammogram and was called back to the hospital a few weeks later for the results. As I arrived at the hospital, I remember thinking I'd only need to pay to park for an hour. Something seemed to take over, and I found myself parking further up the road, where there were no time restrictions.

I walked into the hospital and joined the other women in the waiting room, thinking I'd be in and out within twenty minutes.

I noticed some of the women return to the waiting room after they had seen the doctor. I was praying for them, thinking, 'Oh god, you poor thing. I hope you are OK.'

Just then, my name was called.

DOCTOR: There is a lump in your right breast.

ME: *Pardon?*

DOCTOR: There is a lump in your right breast.

ME: Erm... it was the left one that hurt. Are you sure they're my results?

DOCTOR: Oh yes, sorry – the left one. The lump is in the left one. I'm going to examine you now. Please go behind the curtain and remove your top and bra.

ME: *What?*

I hadn't even thought of asking someone to accompany me to the appointment. It hadn't occurred to me that they would be doing more tests. I was only there to be on the safe side, remember, but now I was wondering where the bloody hell the safe side was.

DOCTOR: You can put your top back on now, and please take a seat back outside. There are lots of other things it could be, and we won't know until we do more tests. We will get you ready for a scan. It is likely just to be a cyst.

ME: Oh, erm – OK, then.

It's probably a cyst, I thought.

I was called back in for the scan.

DOCTOR: Oh yes – it is right there. Can you see it? It is almost perfectly oval, which might be a good sign, but we can't tell from this scan. We will need to do a biopsy.

ME: *Pardon?* What do you mean a biopsy? Why can't you tell from this scan that it is just a cyst?

DOCTOR: We will do it now for you, and then we will write to you when it is time to come back in for the results. It can take around two weeks.

ME: Oh, OK. I might have cancer?

This day has taken an unexpected turn.

When I went back to collect the results two weeks later, I walked into the reception and explained I was there to collect my biopsy results. The guy behind the desk was having a hard time finding my details. Eventually, he said, 'Oh, it's a misread.'

'A *misread*? Are you kidding me?'

When I was in my mid-twenties, my mum found out she had a deficient BRCA gene. She had been tested after the fourth time of having cancer. My brother and I therefore had a fifty-fifty chance of also having the gene mutation. As a young adult, I faced the choice – to get tested for it, or not. Knowing that if I did have the gene mutation there was a significantly increased risk of a cancer diagnosis in my lifetime. If it came back positive, I would be faced with another choice – preventative surgery (mastectomy) or risk doing nothing and hope I got lucky. I decided to get tested.

The DNA team had called me the night before I was due to get my results to say they hadn't been able to get an accurate read and that they would need to try again. Now here I was again with another misread!

RECEPTIONIST: No. It is *Miss Reid* – the doctor's name. She doesn't often work from this hospital. Please head to the waiting room.

Now, I'm pleased to report that I was given the all-clear that day. My genetic results were negative too.

What was it that made me go through with my appointment, despite my dot being very talkative about not needing it, telling me to give it to someone else?

What was it that had me park my car where there was no time limit despite my dot being very sure I would only be twenty minutes?

And look how my dot resurfaced events from fifteen years earlier when I misunderstood *Miss Reid* to mean *misread*!

Can you see how our personal thoughts want to drive our behaviour?

Can you see how something deeper and more intuitive is always available to guide us?

Can you hear that deeper whisper underneath the personal mind nudging us into alignment?

This story shows how I was continuously surrendering my 'know-it-all' dot. It shows how I was listening and following the guidance of the deeper whisper from the white space instead. I was blessed to have the outcome I had. If I hadn't, that willingness to surrender the dot might have been the thing that saved my life. Remember, my dot was *not* going to get tested.

This is what is happening all the time – for all of us. We have access to this built-in, wise navigation system, but the dot constantly tries to override it or decides not to listen, thinking instead that it knows the best route for us (and it often thinks it knows the best route for everyone else too!)

We're not just the dot – we are also the white space. That is the power that flows through us. The infinite intelligence of the white space is our powerful ally.

ACTIVITY: Surrendering *to* your truth instead of surrendering your truth

Hold space for these reflections, add your insights to your notebook and decide what you will implement.

- What is the whisper of the white space wanting you to take notice of, which is being overruled by the personal mind?
- What does your white space want you to create?
- What does it want you to let go of?
- Who does it want you to become?

Consider what you might be willing to do differently this week as you move into alignment with its call. Complete the following sentence stems:

- If I lived with 5% more alignment, I would...
- If I lived with 10% more alignment, I would...
- If I lived with 25% more alignment, I would...

Note: It can be a little confusing sometimes to identify the two voices. Don't worry – with practice you'll start to tune in to what is what. To me, the wisdom of the white space feels like a sense of something – a calm, grounded, expansive knowing. The dot tends to be more noisy, full of analytics and detail and thinks it knows best.

Key insights

- Black dot vs white space: The dot is the personal mind, the white space represents the infinite intelligence of the universe. True wisdom comes from this white space and is a powerful ally available to and within us all.

- To surrender is not to give up or give in. Surrender means to let go of the personal mind's desire to control, in order to access a deeper wisdom from within.

- The dot is the servant, not the master. It is full of assumptions and has a limited vantage point. Let the white space guide you and you will have more impact, not less.

- As we learn to listen to and follow the whisper of the white space, we move into deeper alignment with our true selves and are guided by a more powerful GPS for our lives.

5
Iceberg Right Ahead!

W hy is the dot – our personal mind – so convinced it is right? It's because it has been programmed consistently since before birth. Even in the womb, we are absorbing information. Like an iceberg, there is a whole lot going underneath the surface that we cannot see or touch.

Have the day off, Jack, because the good news is, we don't need saving from this iceberg! (This might be lost on those who haven't watched the movie *Titanic*.) It is going to be helpful to have an understanding of it, though.

Meet your subconscious mind

You may already be familiar with some version of this next illustration, showing our conscious mind as only the tip of the iceberg. The largest part of the iceberg lies underneath the surface. Here you will find all the conditioning and programming that sits in the subconscious mind. These are shaped by the various influences we have been exposed to, including our past experiences, our environments and our upbringing, forming the belief systems we carry with us today.

We're absorbing information constantly, and deposits are being banked in the subconscious. I am told I am shy. Ker-ching! That goes into the subconscious. I feel embarrassed when I get something wrong. Ker-ching! That goes into the subconscious. The more emotionally charged the memory, the more the subconscious deposits it. We see men in leadership roles and women in support roles. Ker-ching! The subconscious stores that. This is why we call it unconscious bias. We are being programmed through what we see, hear and feel all the time without realising it. The subconscious is also called our *unconscious* mind.

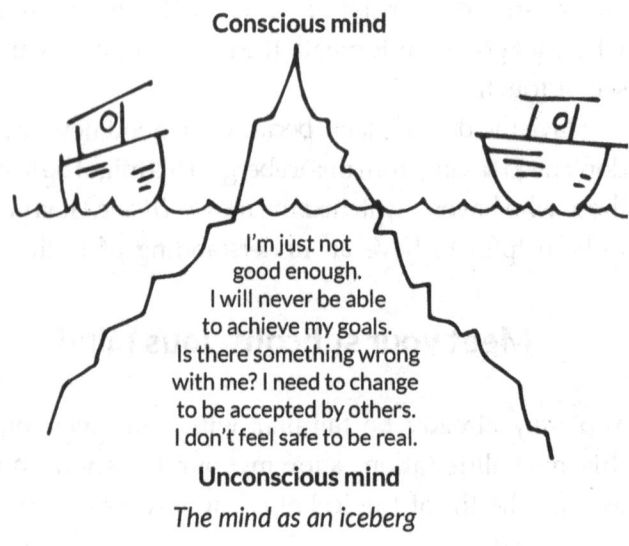

The mind as an iceberg

Most people grasp on an intellectual level that we have a subconscious mind, but most don't truly understand the real significance of how this plays out in their lives. Most people don't *live* from this understanding. Instead, they go about their day on autopilot, unconscious of the set of outdated beliefs driving their daily behaviour. Think of it like breath. I am not always conscious of my breath, yet I am always breathing. Let me highlight this some more, starting with a case study.

CASE STUDY: Infidelity

When Adam was a teenager, he accidentally sent a message to his then-boyfriend. In that message, he was asking someone else for a date. His boyfriend was naturally not happy and dumped him for cheating.

Fifteen years later, Adam was still doing something similar, but this time in his professional life. He was going behind his team's back, lying about his whereabouts and trying to cover up his behaviour. Instead of facing up to what he was doing and having a difficult conversation with his team.

Needless to say, his colleagues found out about his behaviour and dumped him too.

If we don't learn to examine our old habitual beliefs (stored in the subconscious mind) they continue to run the show. We end up with a child running our adult life and we continue to make similar mistakes.

What did Adam learn as a teenager?
If we get caught, we get dumped.
Ker-ching... another deposit made in the subconscious mind. Best not to get caught.
It feels fun to get away with things.
Ker-ching... another deposit made in the subconscious mind. Best to get away with it.
It feels shameful to face dishonest behaviour.
Ker-ching... another deposit made in the subconscious mind. Best to avoid looking at dishonest behaviour.

By default then, his mind might determine that it is better to lie and try to get away with things than face the truth and the uncomfortable feeling that comes with owning up to his behaviours. He is conscious of the fact he is hiding his behaviour. However, he is not aware of the subconscious beliefs that are driving this behaviour.

Question your beliefs

Not only do our own experiences programme our subconscious mind but also the influence of parents, grandparents, guardians, teachers, friends and society all embed certain values and norms within us that shape our belief systems and perceptions of the world. These beliefs unconsciously limit our potential and unknowingly create ceilings in our lives.

When we start to understand the origins of our subconscious beliefs, we can begin to release the grip of them. We start to see that they are not our identity. They are not the truth of who we are – they are simply inherited; they are hand-me-downs. Just like the jumper handed down to us from our older siblings, we can throw them away, knowing we have outgrown them. We can change our old beliefs for more helpful beliefs that better serve our current goals – the desires and the life we want now.

Unravelling inherited beliefs

Knowing this can be so freeing. We can recognise that our current understanding of the world is not actually how the world is. Instead, it is a subjective interpretation that ran on repeat until we believed it to be true. Knowing this can start to free us from our self-imposed constraints. We can start to detach from unhelpful narratives and create a more empowering personal reality.

You can start to see that you are not your thoughts. You have thoughts, but you are not your thoughts.

This is an important point in this book: *Don't marry your thoughts with your identity.* That alone can change your life.

I love to remind people that they weren't born with the labels they have given themselves. They didn't come into the world unable to receive. They weren't born unworthy and undeserving.

You might have learned to believe things and now they're being spoken as if they are the Truth. They aren't. Those labels don't represent your true nature. Your worth is not at stake. Peel back the layers of societal conditioning and learned beliefs to reveal your authentic self, which lies beneath.

Imagine if Adam rewired his beliefs to see that it is OK to be honest with someone if you are not happy in the relationship or the team anymore. Imagine if he rewired his beliefs to know that he could withstand any fallout or reaction from the boyfriend or the team. Imagine if he rewired himself to see himself as a man of courage and integrity. Imagine if he placed more value on that than on avoiding uncomfortable feelings and conversations.

Explore your roots

The following exercise will help you to identify what you saw, heard, felt and read growing up. This isn't only about what you were told – think too about what you were shown. We are being programmed through all of our senses. For example, if someone's dad went to work and their mum stayed at home to look after the house and the children, that will have programmed that person's subconscious mind around gender norms. Even if they were told women work, they were not being shown it. The subconscious mind notices and stores all of that.

ACTIVITY: Examining your subconscious beliefs

Consider the following questions:

- When did you receive love as a child? Were there certain actions, behaviours or accomplishments that seemed to bring love your way?
- How did you learn to get attention from those you loved?
- What were the spoken or unspoken messages about success?
- What did you hear about people with money?
- What were you taught about challenges and mistakes? Were they treated with kindness and encouragement or criticism?

Make a note of what comes up for you.

This can be the start of some deep and enlightening work. As you do this exercise, you might be tempted to blame your parents or guardians for the influences on your belief system. Remember, though, that they're human too. Those people also learned and inherited their belief systems. There is an innocence to all of this, so try as best as you

> can to look through the lens of curiosity and love, not blame and judgement. We're creating freedom and empowerment here.

The road ahead

Sometimes, when people start to get free of their inherited and outdated beliefs, perceived problems no longer seem like problems. Their shift in perspective places them in peaceful acceptance of the situation with no problem to solve. This, of course, is great news. However, it isn't the end of the road. We can still think about what we might want to do next.

Let's say, for example, Katrina has a poor relationship with money and thinks she will never be financially free. She is a high earner but spends all of what she earns. When she was young, her parents always told her there was more than enough. She saw them spending on lavish holidays, luxury interiors and the latest trends. Her friends were always complimenting her on the material possessions she owned.

Katrina realises that her patterns with money were driven by inherited beliefs. This gives her an enormous sense of peace as she can see the innocence of how she adopted those behaviours unconsciously. She is no longer gripped by shame, thinking that she is someone who can't handle money. Problem solved. Shame gone. Realisation made that *'I can't handle money'* is not who she is.

If she wants to create financial freedom, though, she will have to adjust her behaviours and take different actions. Awareness is only the first step. Action comes next.

An analogy I like to use here is of a car that has run out of fuel. The driver is stressed about this until a recovery truck pulls over and tows the car and its driver to the nearest petrol station where the driver fills the car up with fuel. Problem solved. The car now has fuel. However, the driver forgets to drive out of the petrol station. She's at peace knowing she has all the fuel she needs and that her car can run again, yet she is not making use of the fuel.

This illustrates what I see sometimes when people become liberated from their old beliefs. Realising there is nothing they *need* to change, they fall into the misunderstanding that if all is OK, that's the end of the chapter. They stay in the petrol station with their full tank of fuel. What a waste of fuel!

You don't have to *need* something to create it. Your car has wings! Why not go for a drive just because you can?

Fuelled for creation

Don't surrender your truth, surrender to your truth

Learning to create from a place of peace is important because when we habitually ignore our truth, feelings like resentment, anger and frustration start to creep back in. More often than not, these feelings are an invitation to explore a judgement we have on ourselves. It highlights an opportunity to evolve and grow.

Imagine going on a hill walk with a friend, but your friend walks much slower than you. You start to feel some frustration because you wanted to get a good workout in that day. You come back to peace and continue at your friend's pace. However, the niggle of resentment keeps popping back up. You spend the day at your friend's pace and you end up quietly fuming by the end of the hike.

What caused you not to honour your desire for a workout? What is the system you are running that has created or contributed to the result of no workout? Did you sacrifice your desires for a workout to prioritise and please your friend? Did you do it to avoid the discomfort of saying no to them or because you were worried they would get upset or take it personally?

All of life is showing up *for* us, remember? Maybe in this scenario, your growth edge might be to learn to say no to your friend joining you on the hill. Maybe your growth edge is in having difficult conversations. Maybe your growth edge is in not collapsing your truth in service of everyone else's wants – but to speak of and honour what is important to you, even if there is a risk someone will take it personally.

I want you to be the person who can come back to peace, honour their truth in those moments when it wants to be honoured, and create from love, not fear or resentment. How we communicate from peace is very different to how we communicate from fear and resentment.

From peace, you might think to say, *'Hey I really need to get a more intense workout in today, it has been helping me manage my stress levels. I want you to enjoy your hike too so I'm going to run on ahead for a few moments. How about I meet you in thirty minutes at x point on the hike and then we can go to the summit and come down together? Or, if you prefer, have a break here and I'll go for a run then come back and get you in thirty minutes?'*

Or... *'Hey, I'm feeling the urge to pick up the pace – you think we can do that or shall I go on ahead and meet you a little higher up?'*

Or... *'Hey, I think if I'm going to get my high-intensity workout in today, we're going to need to start to head back down soon so I have time to get to the gym – or I could skip the gym and do some hill sprints! What would be your preference?'*

From resentment, you might start to become snappy, sarcastic or distant with your friend.

Remember not to listen to what I am sharing here through the lens of agreeing and disagreeing with what you're reading. The problem with offering up examples is that they can be interpreted as advice, as *the* way to do it. I am not saying that. I am pointing to examples that my white space offers me. Yours might have different ones.

The principles I share in this book are universal and apply to all the different areas of your life. We take ourselves everywhere we go so we are taking the same set of automated beliefs and behaviours with us into our relationships, careers and financial wellbeing. If you find it hard to say 'no', and have people-pleasing tendencies in your social life, how do they play out and impact your family life? Your work life? Your health goals? Your financial goals?

Remember, our thoughts create our feelings. Our feelings shape our behaviour. Our behaviour creates our results. No matter the area of life, this operating system is always at play.

ACTIVITY: Creating from peace

Think of one circumstance that is pulling you away from being centred and calm. Name the emotion that arises from that circumstance. For example:

- I'm angry because...
- I'm frustrated because...
- I'm anxious because...

Complete the sentence by adding the thought behind the emotion (eg I'm angry because... he broke my trust).

Rework the belief or expectation to bring you back to peace. Remember, this isn't about passive acceptance. This is about coming back to a more empowered stance.

Do this by asking yourself:

- Can I let go of the need to control, fix or change this, even just for a moment?
- What growth edge is this inviting you into? That is, is it asking you to develop more patience, less control, more assertiveness or something else?
- What would you like to consciously create around this circumstance in service of your growth?

Reflect:

- How does it feel to create from peace instead of reacting from frustration?
- Where else might this approach serve you in your life?

Key insights

- We are conscious of only a tiny fraction of what is happening within us. Our subconscious mind, on the other hand, is a vast memory bank – quietly storing information given to it through our upbringing, environments and experiences encountered throughout our lifetime. This bank forms our belief systems.

- Our belief systems are the autopilot for our lives. When left unquestioned, they steer our day-to-day behaviours and activities, keeping us locked into old habits and patterns of behaviours that no longer align with who we are or who we want to become.

- We mistakenly identify with our beliefs, taking them on as who we are. We must learn not to marry our beliefs with our identity.

- Knowing beliefs are inherited and don't belong to us can help to loosen the grip they have on us, come back to peace and step into a deeper understanding of our true self.

- This is about understanding, not blaming – those who we inherited our belief systems from, inherited theirs too, and so on.

- Awareness of our belief systems is the first step to liberation, the next step is action. Change requires action.

Emotions such as resentment and frustration can creep in when we consistently deny our own needs for the sake of others. We don't have to forgo our truth. Instead, we can learn to honour our truth and create powerfully from a place of inner peace. You now have an understanding of the fundamental principles of the human operating system and our thought-created worlds. You've gained a glimpse into how we can use thought for us or against us, and you've been introduced to the subconscious mind, along with the voices of the ego and the wise ally, which are always available within us.

Our results are a by-product of our behaviours, which are a reaction to our unquestioned thoughts and feelings. Remember, if you want a different output, change the input.

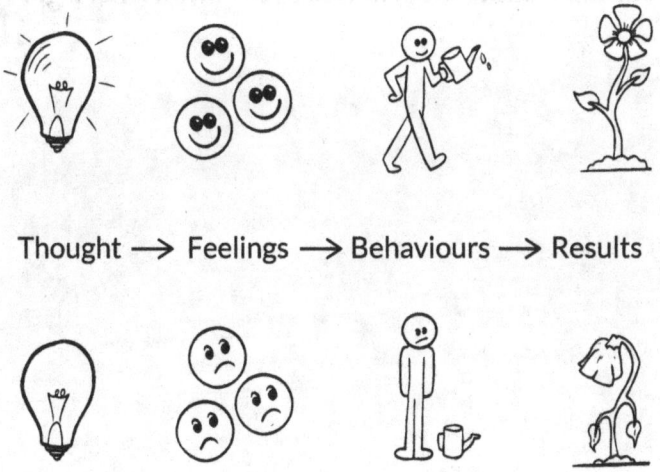

Thought → Feelings → Behaviours → Results

Operating system

Let's bring this understanding to life. It's time to take a more in-depth look at how it is playing out in your world. We'll look too at what you can do to step into higher levels of awareness, gain a deeper connection and trust in your agency, and move into empowered states of being to create and live a life you love.

I've designed thirteen powerful life lessons inspired by my deliberations, and from my work with my coaches and my clients over many years. I've taken all the different influences and blended them into a body of work that will serve your inner journey.

The next part of the book will invite you into stories, reflections and inquiries that will support you to let go of what is no longer serving you and align with your most authentic self. Discovery awaits. Let's go!

PART TWO
THIRTEEN LIFE LESSONS THAT CHANGE THE GAME

PART TWO

Lesson 1
The Game Is Played And Won On The Court, Not From The Spectator Stand

Knowing alone won't change your life. This lesson is all about what will. In this book, we're going to be on the court in two ways: *being* and *doing*. Put differently, we're working on both *the player* and *the game*.

Read for information, inhabit for transformation

This book comes with a caveat. Reading it will have you in the information zone. Finding out lots of nice, juicy, interesting information. However, you need to move to the transformation zone for growth and change to occur. How do you move into the transformation zone? You have to *live* what you are learning.

Life is like tennis that way. It isn't a spectator sport. You can't learn to play the game of tennis well by simply reading a book on tennis. If you want to play well, there will be a requirement to pick your racquet up, get on the court, review the feedback, adjust the play and repeat!

I've done what I can within the format of a book, using stories, reflective prompts and activities to help you live these learnings. It will be up to you to play your part in your change journey, step into action and run some game play for yourself. You deserve to honour your life in this way.

Live your dreams

What stops us from getting on the court? We do! We think our way out of the things we want most, due to worry, fear, small ideas about ourselves and concern about what others will think.

I urge you to be inspired by Bronnie Ware, an Australian nurse, who reports that the most common regret people have at the end of their life is wishing they had been true to themselves rather than living up to other people's expectations.[6] During her time working in palliative care, Bronnie found that most people said they had not even honoured half of their dreams.

---

6   B Ware, Regrets of the Dying Blog, https://bronnieware.com/blog/regrets-of-the-dying, accessed 5 October 2024

I want you now to put your hand on your heart and say *Dear heart, I promise to honour you by getting on the court and playing the game.*

Go on.

I dare you.

Do it!

Even if people are watching, do it silently in your mind. Make that promise to yourself. Don't let your dreams die because of the choices you make or the ones you don't. Your future *will* be shaped by these choices.

An understanding always at work

Whether or not you made that promise to your heart, this understanding of how we work (that we dove into in Part One) is always at play. Your thinking is always creating your experience of life. Your thinking is what will keep you feeling stuck in the stands. Your thinking is also what will empower you to get on the court. You can cultivate a belief system that will propel you forward and have you in action that previously felt impossible and unimaginable for you. How you choose to use your mind is going to be down to you.

Remember how I said thinking is like breath? Breathing (like thinking) is always happening, whether we are conscious of it or not. When we bring conscious awareness to the breath, it can have an incredible impact on our bodies. Similarly, mastering how we use the superpower that is our mind, starts with bringing conscious awareness to it, as the first step. What is the default radio station you're tuned in to in your mind?

Are you full of self-love and possibility? Do you hear a lot of judgement on yourself and/or others? How do you notice you react when you believe that story playing on the radio? How do you then react to how you reacted? You can talk yourself in to the game or out of it. Which will it be?

I'll give you a heads-up before we go any further. Your ego isn't always going to like this awareness malarkey, so it might kick up a fuss as you head towards the court. You will likely feel that in your body. Up until now, it might have been getting away with convincing you of a lot of things without you being conscious of it! It is important to know, though, that the ego isn't your enemy, just a worried friend that is a little misguided and would benefit from your loving help to see more clearly.

Let me share with you an on-the-court example from my life where my ego wanted to drive my behaviour. This story shows how I am on the court in terms of the *game line* – taking action towards my goal of publishing a book – and the *player line* – working on who I am being when the thoughts and feelings swoop in. By not getting wrapped up in the stories my thinking wanted me to believe, I was able to stay on the court and avoid reacting impulsively, maintaining my focus on what mattered.

Don't get too caught up in the context of the story. Instead, look for the messages and the insights that are in here for *you*.

CASE STUDY: Turning things around

I was writing a chapter of this book from a new location. An hour earlier, I'd had a hit of inspiration to bring my laptop and write while visiting a local independent coffee shop. I'd found a place with great reviews that was just a twenty-minute walk away from where I was staying. I'd set up an accountability mastermind, which I needed to report back to on my progress, so I was excited and committed to writing.

I received a warm welcome from the staff. The café had cute, vintage-style décor – an interior that felt like a great space to sit for a few hours and get my thoughts out of my head and onto the screen. However, as I started to type, it wasn't long before I noticed a feeling of annoyance within me.

The acoustics are not conducive to writing. The people behind the counter never stop talking, and their voices carry across the whole café. It is so hard to focus when their voices keep interrupting my train of thought.

What I loved about the staff when I first arrived – their friendliness, their warm welcome – was now starting to irritate me.

Oh, god – now the world's most annoying customer has come in. He is shouting across the café to have a conversation with the staff. Inconsiderate, no respect for others. Why can't he just sit, shut up and enjoy his coffee?

Then the victim thinking reached a new level...

I don't have the time to be faffing about finding somewhere else to write today. I had a goal of getting 2,000 words done, and that isn't looking like it will be happening. Now

I have to walk back for twenty minutes and then find somewhere else, which is going to take more time. Now I'm going to have to rush this coffee and buy another at the next place. I don't want to be drinking this much coffee.

Then my know-it-all voice showed up...

They should put some relaxing music on. They should sort out the acoustics so people's voices don't carry across the whole space. People should be more self-aware and less selfish.

I closed the laptop and was about to leave when I suddenly thought... *Why don't I write about this?*

I opened the laptop back up, and the words flew across the screen. The previously unbearable noise, while I was still aware of it, seemed to dim a little.

The most important line in this story is this one: *I closed the laptop and was about to leave when I suddenly thought... Why don't I write about this?*

Why? I am pinpointing for you the exact thing that occurred, which had me stay on the court and make progress with my book. It isn't something you would be able to see. It isn't tangible. It was happening on the inside.

When I was going to leave, *my mind automatically refocused* on making sure I had packed up all my belongings. In that moment *it automatically let go* of the other thoughts making me want to leave. There was a fraction of a second where *my thinking fell away*. In that fraction of a second, *from that space that had been created within, the idea came to me...* why don't I write about this?

THE GAME IS PLAYED AND WON ON THE COURT

This is what I am pointing you to. This capacity is within us all. When you drop out of your personal mind, new insight will come through. Will you be awake enough to notice it?

Now, spot what I am *not* saying. I am not saying that relaxing music suddenly came on or that suddenly the customer stopped shouting. When he went quiet and then started shouting again, it did interrupt my mind. I did notice, but I got back to capturing this story so much faster because I wasn't keeping my focus on the thoughts that were creating the annoyance. I had redirected my mind to a more helpful thought – *I can use this experience!*

When you learn to change the relationship with your mind's stories, there is so much less to change on the outside. The excuses you're telling yourself about why you can't be on the court, start to fade away.

We can get so much time back this way because we stop solving problems that are not problems other than what the mind has made up. If we don't give ourselves that opportunity to build this relationship within ourselves, we will always be looking to change and control the external environment. We will always be trying to change and control other people. We will always be coming up with excuses. True freedom comes from within.

- Can you see how this internal narrative impacts our lives?
- Can you see how happiness and peace are so much closer than you realise?

- Can you see how the ego mind likes to be right?
- Are you starting to get a sense that it is an inside job?

This book aims to point you to a solution where you can be free, regardless of circumstances. This is a freedom that no one can take from you. This is a freedom that can have you playing your best game yet.

It is time to take a look at where you are positioning yourself – on the court or in the stands. Head over to the activity and let's create your game play.

ACTIVITY: Game time

Make notes on your responses to all of the following questions:

- What would you love to be saying about your life one year from now?
- If you were being radically honest with yourself, where would you say you are being a spectator rather than a player when it comes to making that your reality?
- What is stopping you from getting on the court?
- What is the cost of not getting on the court one year from now?
- Five years from now?
- Ten years from now?
- What would being on the court look like?

- What about this is important to you?
- What is one small step you are willing to take this week that will get you on the court?

Key insights

- Information alone won't create transformation. Transformation requires action. Growth comes from actively applying what you learn.

- Make a promise to yourself to honour your life. Many people's greatest regret is not staying true to their dreams.

- The choices you make and don't make shape your future. There is a cost to remaining in the stands.

- Thinking is like breath – it is always happening whether we are conscious of it or not.

- Bringing a conscious awareness to something can have an incredible impact. Notice the radio station running in your mind. What are you tuned in to? You can talk yourself into the game or out of it.

- When we get on the court and step into action, our thoughts will be triggered by events, circumstances and people around us. That is life showing up *for* us.

- Be the player that takes action. Be the player that challenges their judgements and assumptions. Be the player that redirects their mind – choosing more empowering thoughts will keep you on the court for longer and focused on what truly matters.

- Freedom from within comes from switching up internal narratives, not external conditions. This is a freedom no one can take from you, and it will save you both time and energy.

- When your thinking falls away, you open up for insight. Are you awake enough to notice?

Lesson 2
Be The Creator, Not The Victim

Steve Chandler said, 'Owners focus on what they want. Victims focus on what they fear. And both positions are pure internal invention.'[7]

In this lesson, let's take a look at this powerful distinction, which can shine some light on the way you look at the world and how this might impact your experience and your results.

Embracing the future

I have hired many coaches to support my growth over the years, and there are so many unforgettable, standout moments that have caused significant shifts

---

7   S Chandler, *Reinventing Yourself: How to become the person you've always wanted to be* (The Career Press, 2005)

for the better in my life. The work I have done with my coaches is evident throughout this entire book. I simply would not see the world the way I do without the journey I have been on with those coaches, and I wouldn't be the person I am today.

There are two coaching moments I will remember forever. Both of these resulted from some of the most challenging circumstances I have faced. I will share one of those coaching moments later in the book. Here is the first one.

CASE STUDY: Becoming the creator

I was having a session with my coach Carolyn, just after I had received an unexpected business invoice for a multiple five-figure sum, along with a note that there would be a hefty interest charge if the invoice was not paid within a short time.

Carolyn said to me: 'Lisa, this is your opportunity to see expansion in the face of adversity.'

To some, these words – or another version of them – may have been heard before and sounded like cliché advice. When your ego mind races past the gold in the words, without really hearing them, you might immediately think, *Yes, yes, I know that, but...* Even now you may have read them quickly and not taken them in at all or thought that they're nothing mind-blowing.

However, for me, the words landed right in my heart. I felt the full force of them. This was the most loving invitation. This was an invitation to connect me back to my power. To remember my agency to create. To step into a position of authorship in my life and away from the position of victim. My coach offered them up to me as an act of service. She knew the power available within me, and she was not there to entertain small ideas about me. She was there to wake me up to the giant within.

This is one of the most significant differences between a coaching conversation and a conversation with a friend. Carolyn's words cut right through the story I was telling myself. It redirected my mind away from its sob story and righteousness, and into focus, resourcefulness and creativity. No one was coming to save me, and I didn't need them to. She was reminding me of my capacity to save myself.

Now, I didn't have the money lying around to pay that invoice; not that many years before, it would have been my entire salary. It certainly wasn't an insignificant number to me at the time. However, I rolled my sleeves up and got to creating the money. Instead of allowing all my old thoughts and habits to run the show and limit me, I decided to lean into a different way of being, one that put the focus on my creativity rather than on any lack. No attention went to the feelings of righteousness; instead, I stepped into what would truly serve me in that moment – to get to work and come up with fun ways to serve people. When my mind wanted to divert back to righteousness, awareness allowed me to notice it, be with it for a moment, and simply come back to creation.

The truth is that time spent complaining and getting people to feel sorry for how tough things are for you is not going to get you out of the hole. It would be easy to enrol my friends in my hardship and the audacity of my supplier to land me with this bill in this way – to get them on my side as I relayed the facts about how I had specifically asked them to make sure this didn't happen, how wrong they were to do this to me, how unprofessional and inconsiderate it was to email this news to me like it was nothing. That would not have helped me in the grand scheme of things, though. It would have just reinforced the 'gain' I received from a victim-being state. (More on this in Lesson 6, 'Identifying Secondary Gains'.)

Don't get me wrong – we all need friends to listen and allow us space to sulk from time to time. It can feel therapeutic for us to have friends agree with us, validate our opinions and make us feel better. A good sulk can be quite healing at times. The problem starts to occur, though, if this way of relating to things becomes the context for our life. Sulking, complaining and sob stories are not ideal go-to states if you want to have a happier, more peaceful and soul-nourishing life. Have a few minutes to get it out of your system, and then embrace a different perspective, so you can let go of your complaint.

What I sense my coach was seeing back then was that this 'victim position' was a bit of a context for my life. I often didn't believe I could create quickly or create big. I did slip into those old behaviours when something looked impossible – behaviours that were in tune with thinking that I was helpless against those circumstances. Carolyn therefore said the one thing that invited me to see myself differently and take me right out of that position of helpless victim. She invited me into a new possibility and a new way of thinking.

BE THE CREATOR, NOT THE VICTIM

After we'd come up with a few next steps to make the money, Carolyn decided she would help me evolve even further.

CAROLYN: You could apologise to them.

ME: *What? Me? Apologise to them? For what?* I haven't sent them a bloody bill. They are the ones in the wrong here.

CAROLYN: Well, if you want to have a graceful exit, you have some relationship-building to do, and an apology might soften them. It might not, but is it worth trying?

ME: What do I have to apologise about?

CAROLYN: Well, from what you've shared, might they think you're a bit of a pain-in-the-ass client, always asking questions? Might they see that as you questioning their abilities? Might you be taking up a lot of their time?

From my perspective, I was asking questions so that I could learn, as their area of expertise was not an area I knew much about. From their perspective, maybe they felt like they weren't being allowed to just get on with their work.

CAROLYN: You could say, 'I can see how I might be a pain-in-the-ass client. I'm sorry for that. Let's agree on the best way to communicate going forward so that we can get the remaining body of work completed and part ways as smoothly as possible.' That might be enough to create a little bit of softening.

ME: *Fine!*

Removing the ceiling

From stepping out onto the court in this experience, I learned how powerful a creator I am. I say this not from a place of arrogance but from a place of love. This experience taught me what I was capable of when I wasn't focusing on, and worrying about, the thoughts of the victim mind. I was willing to be on the court, taking action to make that money, and I was willing to take another look at the previously unquestioned stories the victim mind had convinced me were true. I chose to *be* the creator from that moment. I didn't wait until it felt believable.

Each time an unhelpful thought popped up, I acknowledged its presence and refocused with a question, *What is the next thing I need to do to create that money?* I kept coming back to presence and then taking an aligned action. It was a consistent practice and it required a devotion to the practice.

I got to see how much is possible when we focus our energy and attention on the things that make the difference. I've seen massive shifts in my own personal leadership of my life, and I've experienced how great it feels to be proud of your actions and behaviours in challenging circumstances.

It wasn't that the other voice immediately died down. Believe me – my ego wanted to communicate a lot about my supplier and how it wasn't my fault. It had a lot to say about not letting them think they were right. It took strength for me to override that voice and to come from a deeper connection to myself.

When Carolyn invited me to apologise, I did not think at the time *Oh, how wonderful, Carolyn is helping me evolve even further.* I thought, *Huh? What? Maybe Carolyn didn't hear me. Carolyn, are you not hearing me? They are the problem – it's them, not me!* But I trusted her, and I wanted to be free, so I was willing to listen and run the experiment.

I apologised. I apologised with integrity, and it felt good to show myself that I was the person who could do that, even with all the discomfort. It felt good to show myself that I was bigger than my feelings. It felt good prioritising a way of being that made me proud rather than a way of being that was solely focused on being *'right'*.

Did my apology soften them? No, not really, but that is not the point. In this scenario, the best thing was ultimately to exit the relationship. This book isn't about tolerating things that aren't working well. It is about who you are learning to be and showing up as your best self throughout all circumstances.

This is about working on the player. This is about your relationship with yourself – the most important relationship of all. Are you willing to work on your blind spots in service of your freedom and growth? Are you willing to let go of the thoughts of the ego and allow your expression to come from your higher self? Are you willing to be in a little discomfort in service of your evolution?

> **ACTIVITY:** *Being* **the creator**
>
> 1. Reflect on a recent situation where you felt contracted or limited. Note it down.
> 2. Write down any beliefs that might have contributed to that feeling.
> 3. Meditating on this scenario, mark where you would score yourself on a scale of 1 (victim) to 10 (creator).
> 4. Ask yourself, *What would someone in the creator position think, feel, say or do about this?* Write down your answers.
> 5. Answer these questions: What am I willing to implement from the answers that came? Who or what might support me with this? How might I create that support for myself?

One thing that helps me to move into a higher vibe of creator energy is recognising what I already have and who I already am. That's coming up next.

Key insights

- Owners focus on what they want. Victims focus on what they fear. Both positions are pure internal inventions.

- A slowed-down mind can listen better and will hear the gold in the words being offered to it. A mind led by ego will race past without even noticing the invitation.

- A pity party might feel good to your ego in the moment, but it won't help you in the long run – fulfilment does not come from pity.

- It is an act of service to step into a position of authorship of your life, and it can be so gratifying to work on you – the player. Be willing to get uncomfortable in service of making a greater contribution.

- Give yourself the chance to realise how powerful you are. Don't wait until it feels believable.

- Freedom lies in daring to see yourself and life from new perspectives. Be bold enough to run a few experiments along the way.

- Your relationship with yourself is foundational. Embracing challenges from the perspective of the creator will foster a deep self-trust and a capacity to handle challenges with commitment and grace.

Lesson 3
Becoming Lucky

When someone says to you *You're so lucky*, what do you feel? The ego mind can show up in funny places, and this was a place where it was showing up in me. I used to hear the words and feel annoyed because it felt like someone was diminishing my hard work. But remember: feelings are not facts, so what is the deeper truth here?

Are you resistant to being lucky?

I had a resistance to being lucky for most of my adult life. Whenever anyone said *You're so lucky* or *It's OK for you*, I stopped listening well to anything they would say next. Instead, I was listening to the workings of my mind.

Statements like *'You're so lucky that you love what you do'* or *'It's all right for you because you know what you want'* were usually met (in my mind) with *'Excuuuuuuuuse me? Do you know how many jobs I have had? Do you know how many risks I have taken? Do you know what I have given up? Do you know what I have lost? Do you know how many times I have had to take a lower salary and start again? Do you know what it has taken to be able to love what I do? You're not willing to take risks; you just want to complain and not do anything about it.'*

First came the defensiveness and then the attack. The politest thing that could come out of my mouth at times like this was, *Oh, it's not luck. I have worked for it.*

Sometimes I would even go as far as to verbally list the many times I have had bad luck, just so that they knew that I was not lucky and that they were, in fact, out of order for making that assumption. My ego loved this – this race to the bottom, this expression of *Look how hard it is for me.* I mean, how can you be a hero if you haven't had any hardship, right?

Of course, there is a truth to the *I have worked for it* statement. I have been willing to follow the path that often seemed illogical. I have halved my salary and started again, only to discover that wasn't what I wanted to do either. I have navigated *many* doubts, fears and anxieties. I have invested more than many would spend on a house in my own personal and professional growth, without knowing if any of it would see a return. I have embraced living in uncertainty. I have bet on myself, I have put myself out there, and I have been judged, criticised and told who I am, what I think and what I should and shouldn't do.

Then, one day as I was immersed in reading about the habits and minds of investors, here's what jumped out at me: I *am* lucky! Oh my god, am I lucky. That is actually true.

The and/or distinction

I realised I was in denial about luck because I believed, on some level, that it discredited what I had done. Luck is passive and therefore nothing I could claim as my doing. Luck wasn't personal enough – it means things are given, not earned and therefore not respected. Not by me or by others. I felt that when people saw me as lucky, they missed all the other stuff I have done that I've worked bloody hard for. I thought when luck was involved, hard work didn't count.

Then I gained a new insight that allowed me to drop the resistance to being seen as lucky. I can be lucky *and* I can have earned my stripes. Both can coexist, and one does not devalue the other. I felt moved to start my day by writing out all the things that I was now free to own around my lucky nature. I just allowed the pen to meet the paper and see what came through – free writing, as some people call it. I wrote this:

'I am lucky. I am lucky to have been born into this body, this family, this life. I am lucky to be a white, straight woman in a society that is relatively accepting and accommodating of white, straight women. I am lucky to be able to read, write, hear, smell and speak. I am lucky to have a fully functioning body. I am lucky to have an intuitive nature. I am lucky to have everything I need and more. I am lucky to be in life-changing conversations. I am lucky to have received an education. I am lucky to have knowledge and creativity. I am lucky to be supported and loved. I am lucky to have a strong community. I am lucky to have people who care about me. I am lucky to have never known first-hand, extreme violence, drugs or terror. I am lucky to have been born into the western world. I am lucky to be able to access clean, safe drinking water. I am lucky to have all these things ready and available to me simply because I was born into this life, into this body and these circumstances. I am lucky and blessed, and I will never be resistant to being seen as lucky again. This moment is fuller, richer, brighter than my thinking mind can ever allow me to see and notice. I am lucky – so lucky – because I didn't do anything to receive all of this. I am lucky and I am beyond humbled and grateful for that.'

How luck matters

What difference does it make, knowing that I am lucky?

Well, what I can share for now is that I moved instantly into a new feeling – a higher level of vibration and a deeper connection to the joy of being alive. It was a more relaxed feeling, knowing it wasn't all on me to find ways to meet my needs. I knew that something more powerful was already providing. I can be loving and present with someone who tells me I am lucky, without feeling the need to defend myself or correct them, because there is nothing to defend or correct. I am lucky, and I wholeheartedly feel the blessing of that. I feel a deeper sense of presence and appreciation, and a deeper desire to have my life count in meaningful ways. I've been given all these gifts. It is my duty to use them well.

Aren't we all looking for a better feeling? Isn't that what happiness is? The universe provides for us in abundance. I simply hadn't been ready to own that truth. I had thought my annoyance was a result of other people not seeing me. This new acceptance made me realise *I* wasn't seeing myself.

Why is this such a game-changing lesson? What we focus on grows. You have likely heard of the law of attraction. We are energetic beings that attract and repel from a frequency we emit. Polarity thinking can keep us trapped. We don't have to fight for one position or another – both perspectives can dance harmoniously together. I encourage you to run the experiment and see what reasons you discover for yourself – reasons that you are lucky.

This map of the world isn't about being a Pollyanna. This is about slowing down and appreciating what we already have. The impact of looking out at life in this way is enormous. It enables us to appreciate and hang out in the present moment. To see beauty all around us. To not take for granted what we have. So much of our mind and our society wants to focus on lack, on what's missing, on what's wrong or what's next. Take a moment to see how lucky you are.

> **ACTIVITY: Being lucky**
>
> Grab your journal and write for a minimum of ten minutes.
>
> Start with 'I am lucky because...' Use the prompt questions below if you need some help to get the cogs turning.
>
> - What have you been blessed with that you didn't need to do anything for?
> - Who has supported or guided you in life and who has shown you love and kindness?
> - What natural gifts and inner qualities do you have?
> - What experiences have you received that have shaped you in meaningful ways?
>
> Once you are complete, reflect on the below:
>
> - How has connecting to this deeper truth changed your feeling within?

Key insights

- Polarity thinking can trigger defensiveness. Embracing the *and* mindset helps us see that two things can coexist – such as luck *and* hard work.

- Embracing luck does not mean invalidating our hard work. We can honour our efforts while appreciating all that supports our journey. It doesn't negate our dedication; it opens us up to a deeper truth.

- Embracing luck recognises that while we are a creator, we are also a receiver. When we let go of the need for validation and credit, we open up to a deeper appreciation for life, knowing that it is not all on us to provide.

- As energetic beings, like attracts like, and what we focus on grows. We can access a nicer feeling and a higher vibration when we go beyond the restrictive stories of the personal mind.

- When we take a slowed-down moment to connect to what we have and who we are underneath, we find we have an abundance of evidence right in plain sight for us to sink our hearts into about how lucky and blessed we are.

Lesson 4

What Is Here Vs What We Think Is Here Vs What We Think About What We Think Is Here

If you're not quite convinced of the idea that you are lucky yet, that's OK. I've put this lesson here because I get what it feels like to be in resistance to something, and how embracing a point of view, a perspective or a statement that doesn't feel true for you, can feel inauthentic. When integrity, authenticity and honesty are your values, forcing a new point of view can *feel* like we are acting out of alignment with our values and our truth.

First, remember what I said about feelings not being facts. I will keep reminding you of this!

Next, this lesson is going to do three things:

1. It is going to help you cultivate the possibility of owning that you are lucky.

2. It is going to help you shift into those higher-frequency vibrations and feelings we talked about in the last chapter, whether or not you think and believe you are lucky.

3. It is going to help you release inaccurate perspectives.

When we stay open to seeing a different, more liberating perspective, we have the best chance of seeing it when it is right in front of us. If we are closed, we simply see what the ego wants to see, and not much beyond. In this lesson, I am encouraging you to be open to the possibility that you are luckier than you currently realise.

A fresh look at gratitude

One route to connect to your lucky nature is to adopt a gratitude practice, which can be embodied without investing huge amounts of time. Gratitude is a state of being that can flow through you into everything you are already doing. It is less of a thing to do and more of a place to come from. It can take some intentional practice to cultivate that being state, and I truly believe it is worth it. Seeing the world through the lens of appreciation and beauty is a lot more enjoyable than listening to the radio station of the victim mind.

For example, early one morning I was sitting at my desk with my coffee and my laptop, getting wrapped up in a story of how much I had to do and the pressure of deadlines. Then, suddenly, that story fell away and in that space, I noticed the sound of birds singing outside. I paused to appreciate the beauty in that moment, in life's creations, in the awesomeness of this natural world. Wow, this incredible life force is happening all around me. Miracles are happening all around me. We miss all these moments when we are wrapped up in the stories in our minds. We miss the beauty of life. I paused to be with the moment. I then took that nicer feeling into the rest of my day, into my work, into my deadlines. It completely altered how I experienced my day. I was calmer, more relaxed, more productive. I was grateful for it all.

I'm going to explain how you can cultivate that being state if you feel disconnected from it or it isn't your go-to state, starting with a personal experience of mine.

CASE STUDY: Recognising value

In my second year of living in Vancouver, I was missing my circle of friends. I had moved from London, where I had a good bunch of gal pals, back to Scotland just before the Covid pandemic and the first lockdown. Admittedly, I hadn't given Glasgow a chance before I decided to head to Vancouver and see if it was somewhere I wanted to relocate to.

I set off for a summer in Vancouver in 2022, then decided I needed to try it out for longer before making any residency applications. I loved my summertime adventures there, but things felt different when I returned in January 2023. This time I was bouncing around from Airbnb to Airbnb and felt unsettled. I was in Vancouver, then LA, then Phoenix, then Sedona, back to LA, over to Salt Spring Island and then back to Vancouver. Because I had no permanent base, I was finding it hard to grow a community in Canada.

I was sitting on the couch one day feeling isolated and thinking to myself, *I don't have any friends. I have no one that I am a priority for.* Then I got out a notebook, and I listed all of the friends I had in my life. It filled pages and pages. I'm not talking about people I know on Facebook that I've never met or spoken to – I'm talking about friendships I have formed over the years.

What I saw was that I had the most incredible people in my life. I had strong friendships all over the world because of the nomadic lifestyle I had adopted in my twenties, and many of those connections were still in my life in one form or another. Of course, I can't see them all the time when we live in different countries, but this exercise slowed my mind down. It brought my mind out of its loneliness story into one of a full heart and relaxed deep appreciation for who I am, what I have and the people in my life.

I saw that there was nothing wrong with me. I wasn't not wanted – I just had a system that meant my friends were worldwide, not on my doorstep. Questioning the story and going to work on showcasing the reality moved me out of pain and into a place of heartfelt gratitude and deep appreciation.

This story illustrates the huge differences between:

- What is here (in my case: I have lots of friends)
- What we think is here (I have no friends)

- What we think about what we think is here (no friends = not loveable, not important)

Can you see why this distinction between the three matters? Can you see how important it is to be accurate? When I became accurate about the facts, my heart went from empty to full in an instant, without any external circumstances changing.

Know that this distinction applies far beyond this particular subject matter on our lucky nature. This distinction between the three phrases is key to building and maintaining healthy relationships and explaining why they fall apart. You'll see this laid out for you in a powerful way in Lesson 9 – Forgiveness (fact vs story).

Remember what I shared earlier in the book about peace not always being the final destination? This Vancouver story is a great example of that. This process had me come back to a heart at peace, and in the stillness, I knew what to do. My heart is so full of love for who I am and what I have, *and* it also desires in-person connection and community. I knew it was time to return to the UK and complete this Vancouver chapter of my life.

Higher vibes

I was creating my return from a full cup. From a feeling of joy and vibrancy. From the aliveness of the creator-being state. No part of me felt like I had failed by returning to the UK. No part of me felt like I was giving up or that I had made a mistake trying out Vancouver. No part of me felt like this was a step backwards. My decision came simply from peace, love and clarity, and it was the obvious next step. I have emphasised this here because so many people are afraid of trying things out for fear of failure and fear of the unknown.

Many people are afraid of how it will look if their plans don't work out. In my case, the absence of that negative, critical inner narrative was so striking to me. It also hasn't always been that way. I've shared my Vancouver story to fly the flag of possibility for you and your inner dialogue. At times the dialogue will still surface, and who cares if it does? If you're implementing the understanding and lessons I am sharing with you in this book, you're going to start to relate differently to your inner dialogue so you don't grip onto it so tightly. Then there will be many other times when it will not even show up at all.

Use this Vancouver experience to inspire you. Get into a practice of separating any story you may be wrapped up in from the reality of your situation, and notice how much of a difference this starts to make in your levels of inner peace and happiness. Notice what insights you receive from a peaceful state. Notice the wisdom that comes through from a quiet mind. Notice where you are being guided to from love.

Cultivating a mind–body–spirit connection daily will make you feel blessed and loved and capable of more than ever before. I've done a lot of deep work over the years to be able to share with you the kind of transformations that have occurred for me.

WHAT IS HERE VS WHAT WE THINK IS HERE

Know that this is the start, not the end, and be patient with yourself as you embrace these lessons and practices.

The following exercise is a simple and effective way of cultivating an appreciative, grounded state of being.

ACTIVITY: Being grateful

This is an activity to do right before bedtime. Think about a person, a pet or an experience that you love. Spend time with that person, animal or experience in your mind, allowing yourself to sink into the feelings you experience.

Grab your journal and complete the sentence stem: **Three things that went well today are...**

Those things might have nothing to do with the person, animal or experience you are thinking of – that is just to move you into a loving feeling as you look out at your day gone by.

Do this every bedtime until you have filled a whole notebook. Then, do it some more!

I encourage you to include internal wins into the mix too, not just external wins.

An alternative and fun way of doing this is to grab a big jar and, each night, write your wins on a small piece of paper and deposit them in the jar, then at the end of each month/quarter/year spend time in acknowledgement with yourself and all those wins!

Key insights

- We have a lot to be grateful for, but if we want to be right about what we think is here, instead of getting accurate about what is here, we will miss it. Stay open to new perspectives and you will have the best chance of seeing them. Would you rather be right, or free?

- Gratitude is a way of life. A place to come *from*. Not a thing *to do*.

- Much of the time, becoming accurate about what is here instead of becoming attached to what we *think* is here (and then adding in all the layers of what we think about that) is more than enough to shift us into a different feeling state.

- Miracles are happening all around us, and within us, all the time. This incredible life force energy is always creating. If we could simply drop out of our heads and into the beauty of the present moment, we could take that vibrant energy into our everyday lives.

- The more we cultivate a state of being that is awake to our lucky, blessed nature, the more we will experience life that way. The more we can embrace that all of life is happening *for* us, the more we will see the gift we can be grateful for, even in those more challenging times.

WHAT IS HERE VS WHAT WE THINK IS HERE

- Emotionally charged triggers can be pointing to parts of ourselves that require some love and attention – when we look at the story running, we can uncover the positive intention it holds and create a pathway towards that from a place of wholeness and love.

Lesson 5
You Are The Loving Witness, Not The Thought

Whether or not we have free will to control our thoughts is a hot topic in my profession. Thoughts have such great influence over our lives, so it would be good to have a remote control for them, right? We're about to find out if that wish can be granted.

Can we control our thoughts?

Don't think of a pink elephant.
 Oi – stop it. I said *don't* think of a pink elephant.

The elephant influencer

Seriously... stop thinking of a pink elephant!

Will you behave yourself?

What I am playfully demonstrating here is that we don't get to control the thoughts that come into our awareness. Our environments always influence what we think.

We do have free will, though, over what thoughts we choose to believe, attach to and hold on to. If you choose to use your gift of free will to hold on to a negative thought, you are going to cause yourself suffering.

We can also influence our thoughts, by choosing what we're programming our minds with – the people we surround ourselves with, the books we read, the films we watch, the mentors we learn from, etc. While we don't have full control over every thought that arises – as demonstrated with my pink elephant example – we do have the choice as to what we nurture.

The gift of free will

You likely know that you are not a pink elephant, therefore it is easy not to identify with that thought. There are these other, sticky thoughts, though, that feel much more believable, much closer to home. These can seem harder to drop. The principles remain the same. You are not your thought. You are the witness. Remember what I shared in Part One about witness consciousness – you are the station platform, not the trains. Whether the train is saying *pink elephant* or the train is saying *not deserving*, they are both still simply trains. *They are both thoughts we can choose to watch from a distance rather than taking them on as who we are.* We have the gift of free will to make that choice, and that would be an excellent use of our gift.

Let me explain with a story from my life where, if I could stop thoughts coming in, I sure would have stopped these.

CASE STUDY: January 2024

What a wild ride the start of 2024 was for me. I started the year feeling tired but excited about what was to come. Work was busy, and I was dealing with some of life's curveballs. Even so, I had a good feeling about the year ahead.

Shortly before, I enrolled in a new year-long coaching programme to support me with my personal and business growth plans, along with my bigger vision for the future of the UK School of Coaching and Self-Mastery.

I knew that much of the value of the programme was going to be within my control. I could choose to show up to it in a way that had me receive extreme value. For me, there is always so much freedom in that level of ownership. I trust that I am receiving the most valuable lessons available to me, even if I can't make logical sense of them. I'm a fan of believing in a bigger game plan that I might not even know about yet!

January was not going as planned, though. Each day I felt more and more unwell. I would have temporary moments where I felt re-energised, upbeat and hopeful. Then the next moment I was left with feelings of despair, sadness, stress, irritability and anger. My client sessions were the only consistent space in my day where I was fully present and clear-minded. Everything else was a battle, and it was getting progressively worse.

Mid-January brought snow to Vancouver... and it felt like it was snowing in my head too. I had no clarity of mind, I felt physically weak. I suffered headaches and found myself sobbing for hours and hours. Then came a rage burning inside of me, followed by thoughts of whether I should just give up. I felt like I was swimming so hard to stay afloat, and thoughts kept flooding my mind... *Just stop swimming, let the water take you.*

On 22 January a one-hour call with one of the mentors from my coaching programme ended up lasting for three hours. I could sense how much he was trying to help me, but I couldn't seem to allow the love in. I also felt angry when he said at the end how illuminating he had found the call. I said something like, *I guess I'll have to trust you, then,* but internally, something different was in full swing... *It's no fucking good you finding it illuminating if I don't.* I thought, *That's like someone at basecamp, with a map and a clear view up Everest, saying they're not worried about someone else making the climb. It's fine if you can communicate to that person how to find the next footing in the snowstorm. Otherwise, it's not helpful at all; one step the wrong way and they are dead.*

When the call ended, I walked over to my sofa, curled up into a ball and cried for six hours. I didn't even know why. I knew my mentor had a generous and kind heart, and I knew it wasn't him that had upset me. I knew he was friend not foe. That knowing didn't stop the sobbing, but it did let me know not to worry about it.

I woke up the next day and had to force myself out of bed and into the shower. Thoughts were taking over my mind, telling me to go back to bed, cancel my calls and hide from the world.

Who on earth is this woman? I thought. *Is this just perimenopause that has suddenly ramped up 100 notches?*

Later that afternoon, the aha moment dropped. I remembered that just before Christmas, my doctor had prescribed me a different pill, which I started taking the last week of December.

I got Google on the case. There it was – all these women who had been prescribed the same pill were reporting the same symptoms. Severe mood swings, depression, sadness, relentless crying, suicidal thoughts. The pills went straight into the bin, and I was soon back to my old self. Back to having energy for life. Calm internally and a lover of people.

For these three weeks in January, I could only describe my experience as exactly that – something I was *experiencing*. I had felt huge, bold emotions, and there was an all-too-convincing voice trying to make me believe what it was saying. Thankfully, though, there was also this other sense that none of this was me, that actually, I was completely OK, and that I was in there, watching myself having this experience.

We can often think that the bolder the emotion, the more we need to worry about it, and the more accurate our thinking must be. Instead of worrying and getting all wrapped up in the story, I was just with it. I was experiencing it – allowing the trains to be there. In the stillness of that allowing, the insight came through: *Check your pill.*

The presence of this knowing didn't stop the thoughts or the feelings, and it didn't need to. I could just be with this experience, knowing that it wasn't me, it wasn't permanent and it wasn't even true. This allowed me to see through the illusion of my thinking, my emotions and my behaviours, and to allow a better way forward to reveal itself to me.

When we know that thinking is what causes emotions and physical sensations – if we see we are the witness, not the thought – this can often be enough to allow negative emotions to pass. If all we know to do in those moments is not to trust our thinking – can we do that? Yes, we can.

In those three weeks, I maintained an awareness that allowed me to distance my behaviours from my thoughts. I knew I was more irritable and more closed than usual – I simply couldn't do any better. This experience also gave me an even deeper compassion and connection to others. We are all walking our path – we all face our unique curriculum. Who are we to choose what someone else's 'best' should be? Drop the expectations and sink into curiosity and compassion instead. We can still have boundaries, of course, which I'll cover later in the book.

> **ACTIVITY: Lesson 243 from *A Course in Miracles***
>
> This is quoted from lesson 243 of *A Course in Miracles*. It will take a whole heap of things off your to-do list.
>
> > 'Today I will judge nothing that occurs. I will not think I understand the whole from bits of my perception, which are all that I can see. And so I am relieved of judgments that I cannot make.'[8]
>
> Walk about in the world from this perspective and see how the world now appears to you. Then come back to your notebook and jot down what you noticed without your assumptions and judgements. How did situations and people appear and respond differently to you? How did you appear and respond differently to them?

---

8   H Schucman et al., *A Course in Miracles* (Viking: The Foundation for Inner Peace, 1976)

Key insights

- We do not have *complete* control over the thoughts we become aware of. Environments, language, people, places and events can all trigger thoughts to flow into our conscious mind.
- We can, however, *influence* the quality of our thoughts. By immersing ourselves in communities, environments and languages that empower and uplift us. Be intentional about where you spend your time, who you spend it with and how you relate to your internal narrative.
- If you choose to hold on to a negative thought, you will suffer.
- Whether a thought insists you are a pink elephant or a thought insists you are not deserving, both are simply neutral transient energy.
- While we can't stop a particular thought or emotion from coming in, we can observe our thoughts and emotions without jumping on them as we remember that we are the station platform, not the trains.
- Use the gift of free will to surrender any resistance and judgement on thoughts and emotions. Instead, allow them all to be there and simply notice them. Let yourself realise you are watching them and that they are not *you*.
- We don't get to decide what someone else's best should be.

Lesson 6
Identifying Secondary Gains

Why is it that sometimes when we know better, we don't do better? This lesson will help you to identify secondary gains that might be holding you back from achieving what you most want in life.

Hidden influences

I first heard about secondary gains when I was studying for my NLP (neuro-linguistic programming) practitioner certificate. We were talking about behavioural change, and about what keeps us doing things that don't seem to serve us. The instructor shared an example with us to help us understand the reasons why we do what we do, even if it comes at a cost.

CASE STUDY: Christmas planning

'Anyone else here a last-minute Christmas shopper?', our instructor asked.

A fair few hands went up in the room. Our instructor gave a knowing look and went on to describe the agony of Christmas day for her, where everyone else gave amazing, thoughtful gifts. She was embarrassed to hand out her presents, following her rushed trip into the city to grab whatever was left in the shops on Christmas Eve. She found herself thinking, *Why do I do this every year? Why don't I get more organised and put some thought into it earlier? This is so embarrassing.*

People were laughing as they resonated with what she was saying, seeing her experience play out in their own lives.

'God, people are so smug, aren't they?!' she said with a smile on her face. 'Those smuggy mugs with their gorgeous gifts. Do they not have jobs? Do they not have lives? Why do they have so much time on their hands? Don't they have anything better to do?'

People started chipping in. 'Oh, let me tell you what my sister-in-law did last year,' said one of the other participants, rolling her eyes.

I used to be one of those last-minute Christmas gift shoppers. I remember often being in York, the city where I grew up, on Christmas Eve, grabbing a few bags of gifts before ending up in the pub. I thought it was much cooler to be relaxed about Christmas. I got something from feeling laid-back, and I had a tribe of people around me who thought the same. We were in cahoots with each other, laughing at the control-freak shoppers who took buying gifts and planning so seriously. *What a waste of energy*, I would think.

If I were to start planning and putting thought into people's gifts, I would no longer have the same connection with my tribe. I would have to give up the idea of being laid-back and become one of those people I had previously branded as control freaks. I would have to give up the feeling of belonging and togetherness with this circle of people that made me feel accepted. This was my secondary gain, which kept me in the behaviours that weren't helpful for me anymore.

This is a fun, lightweight example, and don't let that fool you into thinking it isn't a powerful lesson because it is. Secondary gains show up in work, in relationships and all areas of our life. Why? Because we take ourselves and our belief systems everywhere we go.

Secondary gains are the sneaky hidden perks that we get from doing something a certain way, even if it's not the best thing for us. We may know that it would be a great thing to apologise to our partner for snapping at them, but we don't because *'they snapped at me first'*. What might the secondary gain be here? *Being right.* That became more important in that moment than a loving human connection. These *human moments* where we don't show up as our best selves will happen many a time throughout our lifetimes, for all of us, and that's OK. They are here to help us notice what wants healing inside of us. If we are willing to take ownership of these moments, we are embracing the opportunity to elevate our consciousness and become more aware and more awake to our true nature. We become more empowered to make different choices.

Secondary gains are also one of the reasons we're not playing those bigger games in our lives and careers, and why we're not creating the change we say we want to see. They are what puts upper limits on us. For example, a female leader finds herself stuck at an income level of £60k despite opportunities to grow. She realises her secondary gain was tied to feelings of guilt about having more success than her siblings. She had always been brought up in an environment that valued equality so her unconscious beliefs were blocking her next-level life. Working through that and letting go of the secondary gain – of not feeling the guilt – had her smash through that ceiling.

A bigger game doesn't always mean having to add more. You might be a really ambitious, driven, successful individual who is craving to slow down, simplify and do less. However, you get something – a secondary gain – from the accomplishment and other people's opinions of you. Your bigger game might be allowing yourself permission to do less. To step out of the spotlight. To see your worth, regardless of the accolades. Remember that there is no one right way. We're all on our life path with our own curriculum.

Think about it: sticking with what we know can feel safer than stepping out and risking judgement or failure. We therefore get to feel safe and avoid failure. *Gain!*

IDENTIFYING SECONDARY GAINS

There's comfort in the familiar, and sometimes it seems easier to avoid rocking the boat. We get to be comfortable and easeful. *Gain!*

If we want to break free and go for what we want, we've got to be honest about these (often hidden) perceived benefits. When we shine a light on secondary gains, we start to see the reasons we hold ourselves back. Then we can decide. Is it safe to stay still? Is it comfortable to deny what we want? Or do we also then feel frustration, a lack of motivation – and similar emotions – when we are not living in alignment with our truth?

There is a quiet impact to denying your potential that gets louder over time. The question isn't how much it is costing you now, but how much it is costing you in the long run when you realise the life you could have had is no longer going to be. Are your secondary gains worth you dying with your music inside of you? This might sound dramatic, and I am OK with how it sounds. The facts are that tomorrow never comes and people are dying with their music inside. I am here to be a powerful stand for your brilliance to be expressed. What is it time to wake up to?

ACTIVITY: Identifying your secondary gains

Where do you know you are still in the spectator stand, holding back from being on the court? Choose one area you want to be in action on and note it down.

Next, think about the secondary gain that has been keeping you in the stands, and note it down.

Here are some examples:
- Safety from the risk of failure or rejection
- Avoidance of the pressure and responsibility that come with visibility and success
- Comfort, even if that comfort is limiting
- Being likeable (not inciting jealousy or competitive behaviour from others)
- Protection of your ego (not having to confront perceived inadequacies)
- Attention and validation from being a hard worker
- The feeling you get from being right

Now you have awareness of the secondary gain showing up in your life, you get to explore it and see if the gain is worth it. Write answers to all the following questions:

- What is this secondary gain costing you?
- What age will you be in ten years? What will it cost you then?
- What is more important to you than the secondary gain?
- What is becoming clear as you sit with your answers, and what will you do about it?

As you engage with this activity, don't filter what comes through. Just write down your thoughts and notice them. From this process, I got some surprising answers and some real clarity on what is important to me. You might do too!

Key insights

- Secondary gains are the hidden rewards we receive from maintaining unhelpful habits and behaviours. They prevent us from stepping into our potential by placing subtle upper limits on our success.

- Playing a bigger game does not always mean adding more – we are all on our unique paths and a bigger game to one person will mean something else to another.

- The art of recognising our secondary gains, and how they are showing up and playing out, helps us make informed decisions about whether to continue with them or to transcend them.

- The cost of these *'gains'* might be greater than you currently realise when you factor in the compound effect of staying still over time. The impact of denying your potential gets louder over time.

- We have to be honest to become free – reflecting on areas in life where you find yourself holding back can identify the secondary gains playing out and uncover the deeper motivation behind any resistance to change.

Lesson 7
Integrity To Your Word (And The Prison Where You Hold The Key)

To me, integrity is one of the most magnetic personal qualities. There's a confidence, gravitas and momentum that comes from living in alignment with your truth and honouring your word. There is also a big difference between speaking your truth and being forceful with your opinion. Those are two wildly different things. If you want to move towards your heart's desires, speak out what you want to create from love, and then live from a place of integrity to your word. *Be* your word.

Conversely, there is a profound cost to not being in integrity with your word. This cost can ripple out into all areas of your life. It impacts the quality of your relationships, and it impacts your reputation. People start to view you as unreliable, as someone they can't count on. Someone they can't trust. *You* start to view yourself as being unreliable, as someone you can't count on, as someone you can't trust. Relationships break down, including the one we have with ourselves. A lack of integrity puts our confidence and self-esteem at risk.

When you honour your word, you are creating a strong foundation for trust, reliability and meaningful connection. When you realise the truth of who you are, an abundant force of nature, you know there is always enough and that you are always enough, which makes *being* your word much more effortless. Scarcity can make us want to hoard what we have and hide who we're being.

This chapter highlights the difference between who we claim to be and who we are truly showing up as. As I said right at the start of the book, you don't get what you want, you get who you're being.

The importance of integrity

I love being in integrity with my word. Integrity is a cornerstone of trust and respect, and it provides an inner compass point that makes decision-making easy. When I am in alignment with my values and honouring my word, I feel proud of who I am and of how I show up.

I have a background in HR and employee engagement. My colleagues and I would often look at organisational integrity and the *say–do gap* – the difference between what people say they'll do and what they actually do – along with its impact on workforce engagement scores. The smaller the gap, the higher the integrity, and the more engaged the people were. When we look at it this way, integrity can be seen as vital to building and maintaining healthy relationships with ourselves and with others, and to cultivate highly engaged environments. It isn't something to dip in and out of at engagement survey time – it is a way of being for your life.

CASE STUDY: Being your word at crunch time

One morning, I found myself wide awake, with jetlag, at 3 am. A message from my coach at the time popped up on Facebook:

One ticket has become available for a once-in-a-lifetime leadership trip to Antarctica with 150 thought leaders and business owners. We leave in a week. Message me if you want it.

I clicked on the link and looked up all the details – what a trip! What a community of people in attendance too, including Peter Hillary, son of Sir Edmund Hillary, the first man to summit Everest; and Graham Henry, the former New Zealand All Blacks rugby coach (and I love rugby). We would get to learn from scientists and experts about the planet and about how we can use business as a force for good. The doors that the trip could open, the network it would provide. Oh man, I wanted that ticket so badly; and yet I knew exactly who the ticket was for.

A client of mine, David, who I had been working with for a few years, had said to me, 'Lisa, it has been my thirty-year dream to go to the Antarctic, but it costs a five-figure sum. I don't know if it will ever be possible.' At the time I didn't know the specifics of how we would create it exactly, but I held it up as possible and assumed we would do it by having him increase the revenue into his business.

I forwarded the message to him, saying, 'Your answer must be whatever makes sense for you. I am simply asking you to be a powerful *yes* or a powerful *no*. What do you say?' He was in! I was super excited for him, and at the same time, I wanted to be on that trip for myself. Yet, not a single fibre of my being was ever going to do anything different than offer it to David.

This story illustrates integrity to your word. My actions are in alignment with my word, even when it is crunch time. It is easy to be in integrity when the stakes are not high, and often people honour their word until a better offer comes along.

Are you being the person who honours their word in moments like this?

I don't think it is a coincidence that I can honour my word. I don't think it is something I have the capacity for that others don't have access to. I think acting with integrity is a choice because of the level of freedom, love and power I have cultivated internally from living what I am sharing in this book, and from discovering who I truly am.

Let me explain...

In 2022 I turned to my coach and said 'Help me realise who I am.' That was the only brief.

We worked on surrendering the false limiting ideas I had about myself and cultivated a deeper connection to that creator energy we talked about in Lesson 2.

As a result of that, I see myself as someone resourceful, whole and capable, co-creating in partnership with the infinite intelligence of the universe. When you back yourself and that partnership, abundance flows through you as a way of being. From scarcity, lack and not-enoughness, I might have made a different choice when I received the message. I might have seen it as the only option to open doors. From abundance, I can draw my own door. I don't need this one. This door belongs to David.

As it turned out, a second miracle was about to happen: a further ticket became available, which had my name all over it. This photo shows David and me with the penguins of Antarctica.

David and I in Antarctica

The prison of integrity

It would be remiss of me not to speak to the shadow side of making a powerful commitment to your word. This way of living can also come at a cost when we have no flexibility and a rigid outlook on what integrity is and isn't. We can find ourselves imprisoned by our own made-up instructions for ourselves. We find ourselves in the *prison of integrity*.

There is a big difference between honouring your word and keeping your word at all costs.

Honouring vs keeping your word

In June 2024 I was on my way home from the office and landed up unexpectedly on the same train as hundreds of excited Foo Fighter fans, who were heading to a concert in Glasgow's Hampden Park. I got talking to three guys sitting across from me who had tickets for the gig.

It turned out there was supposed to be a fourth guy there, but he was no longer able to make it, so they offered the ticket to me. Imagine – a free ticket, to see a band I love, who hadn't played in Scotland for many years. However, I turned it down. I had other commitments to honour.

I am part of a Peloton community, and we were in the midst of a team challenge. I still had one more ride to do for the week, and it had to be completed that night for the team to get full points.

It may have been a different story if my partner had surprised me with tickets. Then it likely would have been a *Hell yes!* Honouring my word in this scenario could have meant not drinking at the gig and getting the ride done that night when I arrived home, or it could have meant messaging the team to apologise and let them know I wasn't going to be able to complete the final ride.

The point is, I am not hiding my behaviour, and I am considering the scale of the impact it will have on others. This isn't about keeping your word at all costs – there are other ways of honouring it. If we find ourselves hiding our behaviour, it is often a reflection of a judgement we have on ourselves.

I like to commit to a healthy relationship with myself. As I said at the beginning of this chapter, I feel proud of who I am and how I show up. I like myself. Honouring my word is a big part of that, and not just in those moments when it is easy. Some of the most dangerous words to your self-esteem are 'only I will know'. Commit to being your word when no one else is watching. Do this for *you*. Your relationship with yourself is the most important of all.

When integrity can stop you from making a commitment

I find it difficult at times to give my word to something if I'm not sure I can honour it.

At a coaching event in London in 2022, we were asked to write down a powerful commitment. For most of my adult life, I have wanted to design and build a house. I had arrived in my forties and had not yet started on this goal, so it didn't seem this was getting any closer to becoming my reality.

As can happen in some personal development spaces, the energy in the room can get people pumped up and carried away with what they're going to achieve. I found it hard to answer the questions about what I had been saying I wanted but not taking action on, and what I was committing to do about it. I wanted to write down 'build my house', but I couldn't seem to put pen to paper.

The reason I was struggling was because when I say I am going to commit to something, you can count on me to do it. That is the power of my word. That is how high value a promise from me is. With all the other commitments I had, though, I didn't see a way to commit to building a house.

Other people were finding it easy to complete this exercise and were voicing their new plans to the room. I remember being moved by what some people were sharing, and feeling the authenticity and meaning in them. I also remember thinking that some of the people might have been making cavalier commitments. If I were a betting woman, I would have bet my newly built house on some of those commitments not being kept!

Reading this, you might find it easy to spot the way out – *Just write it down, then you don't have to do it* – but that diminishes the power of a commitment. That way of being in your life can damage relationships. Think of times you have experienced shame or guilt. Were many of those times because you felt bad you'd gone against your word?

I wanted a different answer to this stuck position I appeared to be in. Here are two things that have worked for me:

1. Span out

There's a saying that we often overestimate what we can do in a year and underestimate what we can do in three. Well, what if I relaxed the timelines and had my house plans on there as part of my twenty-five-year plan? That instantly felt more doable and something I could commit to. I also relaxed the rules about how it had to look – instead of a grand design built from scratch, it might take a different shape; it could be a renovation of an existing property.

Often we are told that when we are manifesting, we need to be specific about the details because the universe works in absolutes. I also believe, though, that there is a lot of power in having a north star, a general direction and a feeling of possibility, without being overly prescriptive of the result.

I sensed that these two things combined were a good move for me.

2. Ask *What could I do?*

If this chapter resonates with you, you likely have strong values around honesty and integrity to your word. Sometimes, when that value set is strong in us, it can make it more difficult to dream, visualise or feel what we desire, or to even begin to imagine what is possible.

If you can't see how something is possible, and you don't believe in saying you'll do things that you're not going to do, then now you're back in the prison of integrity. How can we say we'll have and do things that we don't believe are possible for us to have and do?

If you are in this situation, here's an exercise I like to do myself and also with my coaching clients: invite people just to think and free write on what they *could* do. This is without the commitment to saying you will do it – you're just playing; you're just in the land of imagination. Channel your inner child and allow your mind to get free and dream. Instead of saying *I will...*, say *I could...*, without any commitment. Your integrity is not up for question because you're not promising anything.

This approach can often be enough to get the cogs turning, to crank up the imagination and to start to dream. The first part of any creation is having the thoughts come to our awareness, and to have the thoughts come into our awareness, we have to unblock any resistance to them. Saying *could* instead of *will* can unlock that resistance.

You are always in integrity with something

Up until now, I have defined integrity as being the alignment between your words and your actions. There is something else I want you to consider.

> You are always in integrity with something.

You are *always* in integrity – that is a fresh way of looking at things. If you truly believe you are not good enough – say, not worthy to be on the trip with those thought leaders, no matter how much you say you want to go to Antarctica – your beliefs and ideas about yourself might make you turn the trip down.

Are you out of integrity because you say you've always wanted to go and now you are saying no? Well, it seems to me like you are in integrity with something. Not with your words but with your thinking about yourself. You are in integrity with your belief system. If you find yourself not doing what you say you will do, what is the belief you carry that might need to be examined?

ACTIVITY: Aligning with integrity

What are you learning from this lesson? Note down your key takeaways.

> Reflect on: Where are you in integrity with your limiting beliefs instead of your word? Consider the following two questions:
>
> 1. What are you not doing that you said you would?
> 2. What are you not doing that your goals require of you?
>
> Next, write answers to the following sentences in your notes:
>
> - What would 5% more integrity to your word look like?
> - Who else might benefit from that?
> - What's the wider impact this increase in honouring your word would make?
>
> Remember to look with love as you explore this. There is no room for blame and judgement here. Love encourages honesty, and honesty is key.

Key insights

- Words have power – a recipe for creation is to speak out what you wish to create, and then honour your word. Live in integrity with this spoken desire. When you live this way, integrity becomes a powerful force moving you forward. We don't get what we want, we get who we're *being. Be* your word.

- A lack of integrity comes at a cost, adversely affecting the quality of your relationships, reputation, results and self-esteem.

- Honouring your word will allow you to build a strong foundation for trust, reliability and meaningful connection. Organisations with the smallest 'say–do gap' have the most engaged teams.

- It is important to recognise the distinction between honouring your word and keeping it at all costs. We become imprisoned by our own idea of integrity when we hold on to it so tightly. Find freedom from the prison by living from abundance, flexibility and wisdom rather than holding on to commitments that no longer serve.

- Hiding our behaviour often reflects a judgement we have on ourselves.

- The most dangerous words to say to yourself are *Only I will know.*

- Unblock the path to making a commitment with two simple and effective approaches: spanning out – extending a timeline to give yourself more space to grow into it – and/or asking 'What *might* I do?' instead of 'What *will* I do?'

- You are always in integrity with something. If you find yourself with a say–do gap, take a look at the beliefs playing out at the heart of this. What thought, feeling or belief are you in integrity with that is keeping you from honouring your word?

Lesson 8
Your Judgements On Others Are Keeping You Stuck

If some strange law was passed making it illegal to write more than one chapter in any book, this would be the one I would write because of the impact it can have when we awaken to it.

Get really present. Refresh your listening that we talked about at the beginning of the book. Set your intention to read and listen from an open, neutral mind. This might well be the gateway to all the freedom you desire.

When we judge others most

I don't think it is a coincidence that when people come to me saying they are afraid of being visible, afraid of being rejected or afraid of failure, they are also the ones who are the harshest critics of others. The most judgemental of others. The ones with the highest expectations of others and with little compassion or understanding for others. Perhaps not always out loud, but there is an internal narrative that is running Critic TV on repeat. Often they are not even aware of how much this channel is running.

The people who I see enjoying life the most and creating the most growth are those who are willing to be on the field, in the game of life, embracing their hearts' desires. They're willing to be messy, to experiment, to come out of hiding. They are the ones who have learned to love themselves more, and they are better at questioning their beliefs and their judgements of others. They are the ones in their lane, not in everyone else's business. They are the ones who know that their innate wellbeing does not depend on what someone else thinks, says or does.

Of course, there will be people who grow and play a bigger game while being critical, judgemental and unkind. Still, there is a difference in energy when we create and grow from love, versus any growth and creation that comes from fear or insecurity. There is a difference in how much we *enjoy* the process when we create and grow from love.

As I have mentioned before, I learned from a young age that I was shy. When it came to the thought of public speaking in one form or another, my whole body was flooded with dread. I would sit there watching other people's presentations, while comparing myself and wishing I was able to do that, to sound like that, to speak like that, to have that level of confidence.

At other times I would be internally narrating a storybook: *Oh gosh; that was embarrassing; She sounds so squeaky; She doesn't look confident; That was cocky; That's not right.* My own beliefs about myself were being projected onto the speakers. When it came to the idea of me being the one speaking up – whether on a stage or in a team meeting – that is when the comparisonitis and the judgement materialised.

You see, there is incongruency when your heart desires one thing and your belief about yourself is telling you otherwise. The higher self knows the expansiveness available to you; the smaller self believes you are something else. My higher self knows its own identity. It knows it has no limits. This feeling of incongruency is an alarm call to wake you up. To take a look at where you are judging yourself and blocking the truth of who you are from being fully expressed.

Why we judge others

Our conditioning and programming run the smaller self, and the smaller self projects this programming and conditioning out onto the world and those around us. For example, we may have learned that to get somewhere in life, we have to work harder, try harder and stop getting things wrong. So that becomes our belief system and our default way of seeing the world. Then we project that belief outwards and judge people who don't work hard – labelling them as lazy, and believing that lazy is worse than not lazy.

If others get things wrong (according to our made-up standards) we judge them, we think and believe they are not good enough, we talk ill of them (whether out loud or in our heads), we give them a bad review (out loud or in our heads). We say things like *I would have done it this way* and *They should have done that*. Our vantage point is so limited and full of assumptions. We cannot possibly be aware of all things, yet we get firmly attached to our view being accurate. Then *we* get worried and fearful about how we are perceived! Can you see how this is creating, embedding and compounding fear and worry within us?

We mistakenly think our opinion is all about someone else. I see these judgements on others as an invitation to look within. To identify the part of us that wants some healing, some love, some freedom. I see them as the miraculous intelligence of the body and mind, waking us up to our opportunity to evolve our souls and connect us back to our true nature – our true selves.

What is blocking your path might not always be obvious. I invite you to learn to sit with yourself lovingly and get curious.

For example, let's say you judge someone for being lazy. You might not believe that you are lazy. You might think *That is not true, Lisa. I know I am not lazy*, therefore that judgement is not a reflection of a judgement on myself.

However, let's say that the 'lazy' person is being paid the same as you (or more), gets the same amount of opportunity as you (or more) or gets the same amount of acknowledgement as you (or more). The judgement you might discover on yourself could be that *I am not being respected. I am not valued. I am not seen.* You might have strong values around fairness and equality – the judgement might be *It is not fair. I am unable to create fairness. I am tolerating being undervalued.* If you stay with the inquiry, it will reveal the insecurities you carry about yourself (and your heart's desires) that require some love and attention. If self-coaching doesn't hit the spot, I highly recommend you get some support with uncovering these. It can be tricky to uncover those deeper layers, and a great coach can most certainly help get you there faster than on your own.

CASE STUDY: Striving for perfection

When I was at Byron Katie's School for The Work in Los Angeles, there were some technical hiccups on one of the days, which caused a delay to one of the sessions. The man sitting next to me started rolling his eyes and telling me about how inefficient the setup was and that it should be more professionally run. There was frustration and impatience in his experience.

Shortly after, that man and I were paired together in a process, which led to a deeply moving experience. I learned about his upbringing and how tough his family had been on him when he got things wrong. He was pushed to strive for excellence and perfection, with no room for error or mistakes throughout his life. This was the behaviour he saw modelled by his father, uncle and older brother, and it was how he learned to receive love. If he was 'good enough' in his family's eyes, he felt loved. If he wasn't, he didn't. No wonder he looked out at the world and Katie's technical team through that lens.

Imagine an upbringing where you receive love only from achieving excellence and perfection. Would you risk putting on an event? Would you risk going on stage? Would you want to go for your wildest dreams, knowing the path ahead was lined with uncertainty, risk, redirections and setbacks?

This is what our unhelpful, unquestioned beliefs are doing to us. They are running our lives, and we are asleep to it. Our opinions are full of assumptions and biases. We don't have all the information – we cannot possibly know everything – yet we think and then act as though we do. We think our opinion is the truth. We have so many opinions on how others should and shouldn't act. We judge all the time, and our actions align with that unquestioned judgement.

How to turn this around

If you can learn to let go of the attachment to your opinions and your judgements, you will find more peace in your heart and more freedom to live your boldest life yet. You will find yourself able to move with ease and grace beyond the fear you used to experience. You'll be able to step up to new challenges you have been too afraid to attempt before.

If we want to have a voice, most people look for strategies. Techniques to command more influence and impact. Public speaking courses. We learn about tonality and storytelling, etc. All of this has its place – there is a skill to learn, and with practice, we can improve our skill level. However, even deeper than that, even more powerful than that, is what is already available to you. This is about coming from an energetic state, and a different state of mind about yourself and others.

If you release the judgements on others, you will be releasing the judgements on yourself. When I say release, this isn't about not experiencing them, and it isn't about not noticing them. It is about releasing your *attachment* to those judgements.

Humans will always judge – it is our nature. Judgements are thoughts, and thoughts are beyond our full control, so please don't think the end goal is to never have a judgement on another. This is about noticing the judgement and being willing to question it – what does it want for *you*, how is it asking *you* to grow?

This way of being will give you a more loving, joyful way of life, and you will find yourself more willing to play your bigger game. This isn't a strategy – it is a way of being that will provide you with the freedom to create and the freedom to be fully expressed and unapologetically you.

> **ACTIVITY: Reasons around judgements**
>
> Reflect on a time when you have judged someone in your life.
>
> What was the judgement? Write your thoughts in your notebook.
>
> Now consider that we don't change the game by controlling everyone around us. Write your answers to the following questions:
>
> - What might your judgement on that person have been highlighting as a judgement on yourself?
> - What do you sense it wants for you and from you?

Key insights

- Our judgements of others reflect the judgements we carry about ourselves. By noticing what judgements we have of others, we can uncover our unresolved insecurities and pain that want some attention and love.

- The judgements we hold are shaped by our conditioning and our past experiences. They are conditioned responses resulting from unquestioned thoughts, beliefs and assumptions.

YOUR JUDGEMENTS ON OTHERS ARE KEEPING YOU STUCK

- Judging others reinforces our fear of being judged, which holds us back from being fully expressed.

- Humans will judge because it is our nature to think, and judgement is simply unquestioned thinking. We don't want or need to eliminate judgement – then we would lose our ability to think.

- Releasing the attachment to a judgement is where the freedom lies for all of us. We don't need to attach to our own judgements or anybody else's judgements. We don't have to believe what you, or others, think.

Lesson 9
Forgiveness

Of all the chapters in this book, this one can seem the most out of reach at times. It is also one of the most liberating. I'm not saying this as universal Truth, with a capital 't'. It is simply my observation of my own relationship with forgiveness and reflects my experience of working with hundreds of clients on their own forgiveness journeys.

I say it can *seem* out of reach because I know that, in the depths of our being, we are unconditional love. Like the sun that is always there, we are always whole. When the stories of our personal mind drop away, what is left? Only love. The truth of who we are is safe in the knowing that everything is here *for* our evolution. Therefore the truth of who we are doesn't create anything that needs forgiving. Only our personal minds do that.

Still, it can seem incredibly challenging to the personal mind to forgive, and the timeline for that happening is not within our total control. Whether we are the one wanting to forgive another, or the one seeking forgiveness from another, we must understand that the timelines for forgiveness are divine. We are not in full control of timings, therefore we cannot judge what someone (including ourselves) should be able to let go of and by when. I do think we can open ourselves up to healing and forgiveness, though. I think we have influence, just not full control.

Accepting new perspectives

We hear lots of phrases and quotes about forgiveness. Many of them have been said so often that we think of them as clichés, which means we can miss the power of what they're inviting us to see.

When I spend time with these phrases, I slow down my mind so I can really be with the words on the page and their invitation to myself and this topic. When I do that, things can start to stir and awaken within me. The key lies in our willingness to try the phrases on. To be curious with them for yourself, for your healing, for your evolution, for your own freedom.

Forgiveness is not *about* the other person.
Forgiveness is not *for* the other person.
Forgiveness is a *gift to yourself*.

If you want to heal the pain of what has caused you hurt but find yourself unwilling to try new perspectives, that's OK too. Can you be open to the possibility of being willing in the future? That is still a great start.

Imagine taking a pair of jeans for a test drive. You're not attached to the pair of jeans – there is no skin off your nose if they fit well or not. Before you purchase them, though, you want to wear them around the house, to the shops, in and out of the car. You want to see how they fit, how the fabric feels, what happens when you sit, when you stretch. You want to know what happens when you wash them, whether the colour fades, and if that's a good thing. Now think about paths and perspectives to forgiveness and try them on like the pair of jeans. While you have a low level of attachment to those perspectives needing to be a perfect fit, adopt a high level of curiosity and noticing. Here are a handful I have used before, and you can allow your own ideas to come to you.

Forgiveness does not mean you are condoning the behaviour.

Everything is here for me.

Everyone is growing in their own way.

Forgiveness is for me, not for the other person.

Learning to forgive

We don't tend to have to look far to find an opportunity to forgive. Sometimes, as we learn more and more about our wiring and programming and why we behave the way we behave, we can look to blame our thoughts, ourselves, our parents, our grandparents and our guardians. We can forget, though, that they were wired unknowingly too.

Thanks to the human design, we have all innocently adopted beliefs without being taught that we don't have to get attached to our beliefs. It is easy to blame someone or something else, and it is easy to beat ourselves up, yet it can feel so tricky to access unconditional love, compassion and empathy for ourselves and others.

If we know it is healing to forgive, then why don't we just do it? If we know we should let the pain go, why can't we? When I refer to healing, I speak about it as my personal and spiritual growth entering a new paradigm. Like a caterpillar becoming a butterfly, a part has to die for the transformation to occur.

There could be several things going on. One thing I kept bumping into was my mind's story that forgiveness would mean accepting the other person's behaviour as OK. No matter how much I understood the words *'Forgiveness does not mean you are condoning the behaviour'*, it just didn't look true to me. When I tried on forgiveness, my mind had made it mean that I had to let go of *You did me wrong*, and I wasn't willing to do that. That wasn't my truth.

I remember being in conversation with my coach around the notion I shared earlier in the book, *Any judgement on someone else is a judgement on myself*. I wanted to explore what it might offer me, so I was willing to try it out as a small-t truth. I switched the statement to some questions, similar to the ones I gave you in Lesson 8:

- Where might this judgement on someone else reflect a judgement on myself?

- Where is the part of me that is hurting from being on the receiving end of this person's behaviour?

- What does that part of me want for me?

One of the behaviours in question in this situation was lying. The person had lied through omission, and by painting a false story, they had created an idea of me that wasn't accurate to others. They had lied to gain financially at a cost to me. When I asked the part of me that was hurting what it wanted, the answer was *justice*. When I asked what was important about that, the underlying value it was desiring was *safety*.

I have always valued safety highly and what was being triggered in the depths of my iceberg was the hurt I felt for women who have been sexually abused. Rapists get away with the most hideous crime, violating a woman's body and then lying about it. They get away with it and repeat offend. Women don't get true justice, and they are often not believed, or they are made to feel they did something to cause the rape.

How dare someone lie to cover up their behaviour and then, even worse, make the innocent party look guilty? All of that was in my iceberg.

I've mentioned throughout this book about how we listen through our conditioning, about how our learned beliefs become a filter for how we listen and how we see the world. When this person was lying through omission and by default making me look like something I wasn't, all of that triggered subconscious memories and made me feel rage. Rage, anger, pain, so much pain.

I need to be clear here: there was no rape or sexual assault involved. What I am saying is that my subconscious mind had generalised and fused the two domains. I lost my hair, I lost sleep, I was stressed. I felt like there was a wolf at my door, bleeding me dry, and there was nothing I could do to protect myself. This was not a fun time for me, and if stress shaves years off your life, I imagine I was paying that price. I wanted to access forgiveness. I wanted to access it so that I could heal myself, and yet it wasn't seeming to be making itself available.

At the time I wasn't conscious of the beliefs creating this response in my body. I didn't know my mind had fused those domains. I was feeling the anger and associating it only with the other person's behaviour. That was until I explored the feeling in conversation with my coach. That conversation woke me up to the unconscious thought patterns creating my personal 'reality'.

Redirecting my mind inwards turned out to be a gateway to a big slice of freedom pie. When I shifted my focus from the blame being out there, on someone else, my ego started to turn on myself. I gave it something else to do. The narrative changed to: *I should have known better. I was stupid to tolerate that for so long. Why didn't I see that coming? I'm obviously a pushover, an idiot. I failed to keep myself safe. I have given everything. Why didn't I protect myself? I was stupid to trust.*

This shift was a big step forward because it moved me towards accountability. I now had something I could work on that didn't require anybody else to be different.

It is important here to note that accountability and ownership are most effective when done with curiosity and compassion rather than blame. I looked lovingly at all these untruths coming from my mind – all the false pictures my mind was creating about me. Then I worked with each one to see through the illusion of them into a deeper truth of who I am. These deeper truths became a manifesto for my life. They became a way of seeing myself that activated and cultivated expansion and joy. One of my favourite things to do is support my clients in creating their manifestos that activate and cultivate their own paradigm shifts.

Apologies

I never received an apology in this scenario, and I am not writing this because I wanted one. I am writing this because there may be some people who do think they need an apology to forgive. However, just as saying sorry can be a hard thing for the ego to do, accepting an apology can be equally difficult for the ego mind. Have you ever noticed that? Even when someone else is saying sorry to you, it isn't always easy to truly receive it.

You might hear the ego say something like, *They don't really mean it; They're not saying it the right way;*

They're only saying it because...; I've heard it all before. You know what? Those statements might even be true. Sometimes an apology is authentic; other times it isn't. Sometimes a person will say sorry and then continue with the hurtful behaviour.

The good news is that all of that is completely irrelevant to forgiveness. It is a mistake to believe our ability to forgive depends on somebody else's actions. Your peace and wellbeing are far too important to place in the hands of another. You are the one who can choose to forgive, in service of your own freedom.

Here's another trick your mind might play on you. On occasion, you might hear the ego jump at the opportunity to use another person's apology to reaffirm your victimhood, to reaffirm how right you are and how wrong they were, to give them some great advice (according to your ego). *I appreciate your apology, and here are the reasons why you were wrong to do that. Here's what I didn't appreciate. Here's everything you did wrong to me. Here's how I would have done it.* I am not saying you can't express yourself. It is not healthy to attach to painful thoughts and try to suppress them. I'm saying use what you are learning in this book, especially in Lessons 8 and 9 around judgements and forgiveness, to transcend the ego mind. It can be transformational to learn how to speak your truth from love – to create conversation and boundaries from love. I'm saying *Let love express, not ego!*

The ego loves to be right and will defend its beliefs to the death. If it doesn't, that is exactly what happens: the death of the ego. If I thought someone was trying to kill me, I'd probably fight back too! Forgiveness is hard when we are attached to our expectations and judgements. It is hard when we misunderstand what forgiveness is. It is hard when we value being right over being free.

When it's hard to forgive

When it seems hard to forgive, I like to learn from others who are more able to forgive. I look for evidence of where someone is suffering from lack of forgiveness and then they find the freedom to forgive. Or where people are walking about in the world being powerful in their forgiveness without compromising their values. Then I get curious about what happened. How did that letting go occur and how was that freedom accessed? How are they now looking out at the world?

CASE STUDY: Story vs fact

One of the most powerful times I have witnessed instant forgiveness was during a training programme. The coach was working with a guy who I will call Will. Will's dad had died thirty years earlier when Will was only eight years old, and his mum remarried a few years later. Will carried a lot of anger and resentment towards his mum and his stepdad.

The coach had Will come up to the front of the room. On a flipchart, the coach drew a line down the middle, with *Fact* on one side and *Story* on the other. She had Will start to tell her about what happened.

WILL: My dad died when I was just a kid, and my mum replaced him straight after. My stepdad didn't want me around, he just wanted my mum to himself.

COACH: That didn't happen.

WILL: What? (Will was annoyed.) How the hell do you know what happened?

COACH: Your dad died.

WILL: Yes.

COACH: That is a fact. Then your mum remarried.

WILL: She replaced my dad.

COACH: No, she didn't replace. Your dad died, and then two years later your mum got married. There is no replacing. There was a death and a marriage.

Mum replaced Dad goes on the Story column; *Mum gets married* goes on the Fact column.

Will seemed reluctant to accept this, but he continued anyway.

WILL: My stepdad ignored me. He didn't want me around.

COACH: No, this is your story about what happened. What are the facts?

This pattern continued for the remainder of Will's sharing. It took a while because Will never got far before being interrupted by the coach as she separated the facts and the story. Will wasn't angry now, despite the picking apart of his recollection of events. He was softening. He was starting to cry. He and the coach had a different dynamic now as he watched the facts and story being illuminated on the page. The dialogue continued, and Will now seemed to be relating differently to his own story.

After a while, the coach asked him, 'Will you contact your stepdad in the break and apologise to him? Will you apologise to him for creating him to be this way, in your mind's eye?'

Will replied, 'Yes.'

After the break, Will came back into the room and shared with the room the conversation he had with his stepdad. Please know as you read this that Will had had zero contact with his stepdad; he hadn't spoken to him in all these years. He'd carried a lot of heavy emotion towards his stepdad up until this point, and now he was ready to apologise to him. Can you feel the magnitude of that? One moment you are burdened and the victim; the next you are lighter and doing the previously unimaginable.

Will was in tears as he recounted to us what his stepdad had said: 'I'm so sorry, your mum asked me to respect your need for privacy and space. She told me you were mourning the loss of your dad and I never wanted you to think I was trying to take his place.'

Will went on to tell us that his stepdad was never ignoring him. He always wanted him and was trying to respect him. Will had also not known about this request from his mum to his stepdad.

Wow. One set of events. Two wildly different experiences.

If Will can do it, I can do it. Where am I in story and not fact? The same invitation goes out to you.

> **ACTIVITY: Finding forgiveness**
>
> Identify an area where you would like to find some peace or forgiveness.
>
> Starting with two columns, just like in the story above, as best you can, separate the story from the facts.
>
> Remove all emotion from the Fact column. Remove anything you are exaggerating from the Fact column. Remove anything you can't remember for sure from the Fact column. Those things can all go in the Story column instead.
>
> What are you noticing that is helpful for you? Make some notes on that too.
>
> Be patient and kind with yourself – this can be courageous inner work. I acknowledge you for being here.

Key insights

- Forgiveness releases the weight we bear of resentment, hurt and anger. It is one of humanity's most incredible traits – a powerful force that can liberate us and set us free.

- We can influence the timeline for forgiveness by cultivating openness, curiosity, love and compassion, but we are not in full control of the timeline for forgiveness. Remove any expectations of when it should and shouldn't happen, whether you are the one seeking forgiveness or wanting to forgive.

- Our interpretation of forgiveness can impact our capacity to forgive. For example, forgiveness is a gift we give to ourselves. It is not about condoning unwanted behaviour.

- When it is hard to forgive another, shifting the focus inward to reveal the unhealed areas (self-judgements) that are contributing to our pain can be a big step towards freedom and the doorway to compassionate self-forgiveness.

- A deeper pain can come from collapsing domains that don't belong together, bringing the emotional baggage of past events into the current circumstances where it doesn't belong. Find some freedom from letting each event stand alone, free from the weight of the past.

- Our true self knows there is nothing to forgive, as it is always whole and unconditionally loving. The wisdom of the true self reminds us that everything is here in service of our growth so there is nothing to forgive.

- Take yourself through the process of removing any *story* until only the facts remain. Remember, our healing, our ability to forgive, does not need an apology to release the pain.

Lesson 10
Tolerating Truth And Radical Self-Love

This chapter explores the importance of truth. Friedrich Nietzsche said, 'The strength of a person's spirit would then be measured by how much "truth" he could tolerate, or more precisely, to what extent he needs to have it diluted, disguised, sweetened, muted, falsified.'[9] This isn't about whether or not we lie to other people – it's about how we need to be honest with ourselves to get the most out of our lives.

---

9   F Nietzsche, *Beyond Good and Evil: Prelude to a philosophy of the future*, translated by WA Kaufmann (Random House USA, 1966)

Understanding our untruths

When I started coaching, I began to see why people lied to themselves. Lies can be an escape route from self-judgement. Lies allow us to avoid. Confronting the truth involves looking at things we don't like about ourselves. Confronting the truth could mean we would need to take action we are afraid of taking. Confronting the truth might mean making choices we are afraid of making.

It is comfortable for us to look at places where we thrive, but can we look at those things we're ashamed or embarrassed to look at? The truth can be hugely uncomfortable when we don't like what we're looking at in the metaphorical mirror – but we are not our thoughts, remember. Don't marry them with your identity.

Think back to what I shared in Lesson 7 about being in integrity with our belief systems. If I was entertaining insecure thinking about myself and comparing myself unfavourably to others, my answer might have been not to go to Antarctica. I might find myself making excuses: *Oh it isn't the right time, Oh I am needed at home.* I wouldn't own the truth that I am a no because I think I am not successful enough and feel intimidated by the people on the trip. I wouldn't own it and I therefore wouldn't be giving myself the chance to overcome these ideas about myself and to become the person who can say yes with their whole heart.

You can't run from yourself. You take yourself everywhere you go! Even if no one else knows that what you're saying isn't the truth, *you* will know. Take ownership. Let go of the judgements. Commit to loving all parts of you. Dial up the love for yourself so you can handle the heat of becoming honest. This is the way to work through any self-limiting ideas about yourself. This is the way to build the strength of your spirit.

Achieving new heights

When I hired my first coach, I was a HR business partner earning a salary of £40k per year, and I had no savings. I went for a consultation with the UK's highest-paid personal coach to the elite. Two hours later, he told me, 'It is £30k to work with me for the year.' Gulp. *Now it just got real. I am not elite, and I am not highly paid.* I owned my truth, though: 'I want to do this, and I don't have the funds. Is there a way to create a payment plan? Can we start with a smaller package?'

I worked with him for six months. It would have been easy to say I couldn't afford it, but that wasn't exactly the truth. I didn't have the money, and no one in my family could loan it to me, but not having the money and not being able to get the money are two different things. I wanted to be an outstanding coach making a meaningful impact and a strong income doing work I loved. I wanted the freedom to create a lifestyle business. I wanted to get out of HR. I wanted it badly enough that pride and ego didn't get a seat at the table. There was no room for excuses.

My truth was that I didn't believe I could do it on my own and I didn't know enough about business, so I owned that I didn't have the money and that I needed the help, and I got curious about whether there was a way to find the money. I bet on this coach being able to support me, and I bet on myself being willing to do what he taught me.

A few days later I found a way to finance the investment. I took out a credit card with a 0% balance for thirty-six months and handed over the first £8k for the first three months of coaching. I will never forget that feeling – I thought my heart was going to fall out of my mouth – but that investment had me be all in. It had me show up in ways I hadn't done before because now I *had* to make it back. No one was available to bail me out, I had never been in debt before, and I was handing my notice in at my HR job. The bridges had been burned.

Now here I am, all these years later, with a six-figure business and a lifestyle that works wonderfully for me. The point I am making here is that if I had decided not to own my truth, to come up with believable reasons like *It isn't the right time*, or *I can't afford it*, or *It will be better to do it on my own*, or *I need to take a training course first*, then I would have turned down the support that was fundamental to making such a strong start to my coaching career.

Adding the fun factor

I encourage you to dial up the fun factor. Sometimes growth can feel so serious, but what if we could be sincere about it without being all heavy and serious? I find it helpful to bring in some fun and lightness when exploring lessons like this one.

People tell me I use the word *fun* in strange places. For me, fun is a place to come from. It embodies a love of learning, growing and expanding – loving the journey and all its highs and lows. I don't find fun. I bring the fun. That is what I have activated and cultivated in me. It is what makes me able to look at myself and own where I am not being fully honest with myself without bashing myself with a stick.

There is still so much I want to achieve. How fun is that to see! I am at peace and in acceptance of what is, and I am motivated to keep creating. Not from a need, but from a place of living and loving life. Fun is an attitude that we can apply to anything. What if it was fun to look at the hard things? What if it was fun to be playful with your inner critic? What if it was fun to heal your shame? I promise you, learn to face these 'truths' so you can shift your way of being, and you will see your life transform.

Finding your true potential

What has developing a tolerance for truth done for me? Well, it has changed my entire life in both big ways and everyday moments. It has given me an inner confidence that allows me to attend events without feeling nervous, a calm that lets me connect with others from a place of love and kindness, and an authenticity I can fully own, which seems to radiate outwards and naturally attract people to me.

I have also:

- Set up my own business, doing only work I love

- Tripled my former corporate HR salary

- Published this book

- Been interviewed for respected publications like *USA TODAY* and *CEO Weekly*

- Partnered with a global giving organisation for communities in need, providing clean water, meals and education

- Travelled to all seven continents

- Deepened my most meaningful relationships

- Become more confident, generous, resilient, loving and at home within myself

Now, don't read this about me, read it about you.

What would you like your list to look like?

What are the excuses your mind comes up with instead of owning the truth? Let these excuses go and find reasons to lean in, not out.

In addition to bringing fun and lightness, the best way I know to tolerate truth is to come from a place of radical self-love and compassion. Imagine writing a list of three things you have been avoiding accepting and then putting on some heart-shaped sunglasses, which only allow you to look at these beliefs through the lens of love, kindness, curiosity and compassion.

When we put those glasses on and take a look, we already know that we're not looking at facts about ourselves. We're exploring ideas we hold about ourselves, and those ideas are up for releasing and letting go. This step is so important – separating yourself from the thoughts you have about yourself.

You are not your thoughts.

You are not the ideas you have about yourself.

You don't have to believe your thoughts.

Your thoughts are not facts.

I am intentionally repeating myself here because it is so important to have you understand these fundamental points.

You are not your past either, so don't be fooled by that lie. Just because you may or may not have done things in the past that you are not proud of, those things are not evidence of who you are. Past behaviour is simply past behaviour, and you can make a different choice at this moment, right now. You might have heard that the best predictor of the future is to look at the past. What a crock of shit that is. It doesn't have to be that way at all. A new future is yours for the creating when you allow yourself to see the deeper truth of who you are.

You don't need to do this *spirit-strengthening* work alone, and you don't need to share your deepest insecurities with people you know. It can take courage to be honest with ourselves at a whole new level. Find yourself a trained professional who can hold a safe space for you to look at your beliefs lovingly together, and for it all to remain confidential.

One day you may find yourself so free that you are excited to share about the days when you ran from yourself. That sharing might ignite in others a possibility for their freedom too. I love being that light for someone. I love the ripple effect of change in this way.

When we are willing to be radically honest with ourselves, we can recognise and clean up the judgements that are driving the behaviour holding us back. When we clean up those layers, we become free to express our infinite potential.

I write from my heart to yours with an invitation to take a look at what wants some loving attention and to get yourself free.

ACTIVITY: Strengthening the spirit

Reflect on a recent situation where you avoided the uncomfortable truth.

Add the name or description of that situation at the top of your notes. Underneath that, create two columns, with the headings:

1. Excuses of the ego
2. The Honest Truth

Populate the first column with the excuses the ego made up to avoid taking action or facing the truth. Then put on your heart-shaped sunglasses and list the real reasons in the second column.

> Finally, think about what or who could support you in confronting the uncomfortable truth and making steps towards positive action that strengthens the spirit!

Key insights

- Profound transformation comes when we embrace the truth, no matter how uncomfortable it feels to hold the mirror up to ourselves.

- Truth in this context means looking at the personal narratives we carry about ourselves and the behaviours playing out without confusing them with who we are. By separating our patterns and behaviours from our identities, we create a safe space to explore with fun and lightness.

- When we uncover these *truths*, we reveal where love is yet to be applied.

- When we prioritise a commitment to what we want, there is no room for pride and ego at the table. Shifting the focus onto what wants to be created instead of how we will look allows for radical honesty to own our needs and challenges – and ask for any support needed.

- Learning to look at ourselves through the lens of radical self-love and compassion is the gateway to accessing a deeper honesty. The gateway to strength. Holding the truth with gentleness allows us to witness those parts that we otherwise would reject.

- When we become honest, we can start to become free. When we become free, we are empowered to achieve new levels of success and joy in life.

Lesson 11
Upgrade Your Questions, Upgrade Your Life

If you want a simple way to upgrade your life, this lesson is for you. Just as nourishing our body with wholesome food has a positive impact on our physical energy levels, what we feed our mind matters too. Nourishing our mind heals our soul and fuels our growth. We can do this by elevating our questions.

For years I was mentored and supported by two hugely experienced clinical psychologists. One of them – I'll call him Richard here – shared the following story with me, which helps illustrate the main point of this chapter.

CASE STUDY: Finding presence

One of Richard's patients was in a state of distress right there in his office. She was bouncing off the walls, screaming in anger.

Richard took a moment to get still and internally asked himself, *What can I do here?*

A thought occurred to him to say 'I have something important to share with you, but I need you to sit down for a second and listen to me, then I'll tell you. I think you're going to love this.'

His patient paused, stopped shouting and screaming, sat down in front of him and said, 'OK.'

Richard continued, 'All you have to do is tell me when you're listening and I'll tell you the secret to all of this. The secret to your wellbeing.'

His patient said 'OK.'

Richard asked, 'Tell me when you think you're present, really listening.'

His patient took a moment and then said, 'OK... now.'

Richard smiled as he said, 'That's the secret.'

Right in front of him, his patient went from extreme yelling and agitation, to complete presence and calm.

That is the secret we are all looking for – presence. Yet we don't realise that it is always already available to us. Every single human being is one thought away from complete presence and happiness when not being influenced, entertained and attached to stories taking them away from peace.

The resistance to this understanding comes because we think it can't be that simple. Yet here it is for us to see. My mentor asked that deeper part of himself – What do I do here? He got still and wisdom came through with an answer. The patient heard something in what he was saying, which allowed the other thoughts to drop away and she came home to complete presence and wellbeing. Therapists had told this patient it could take years to learn how to cope with her illness. Richard saw it wasn't an illness, it was a misunderstanding. He wasn't telling her what to do, he was cultivating a way for her to experience presence right there in that moment.

What if we allowed ourselves to unlearn everything we think we know, just for a moment, and experience a deeper truth?

All of us are doing this all day long – dropping into wellbeing, into presence, into our true selves. To be more accurate, we're not *doing* it – it is simply occurring. It is why I love my work to include educating others on this understanding. Remember the clouds – they pass all on their own. There's less to do than you realise. We only need to allow the surrender of the personal mind and we come home to ourselves.

We can assist that surrender with what I call high-quality questions. Questions that redirect and focus the mind to a new possibility.

In Lesson 2 I told you of two hugely impactful standout moments from the work I have done with my coaches. This is the second one. This was the start of the next level for me, which came at a time when I was ready to embrace it. When the student is ready, the teacher appears.

It started with a high-quality question, a question that had me drop out of my noisy personal mind and victim thinking right back to presence.

CASE STUDY: A new awakening

'What are you tolerating?' asked my coach.

'Huh?' I said.

The question had jolted me out of my story and into presence with such power that I needed to hear it again.

'What are you tolerating?' he repeated.

I realised at that moment that I had been tolerating a lot. I had already known that on some level, but I hadn't been able to *realise* a different way of being.

I shared with my coach all the things that were causing upset.

That part was easy. I had been complaining about them for a while, so they flowed off the tongue.

But when he asked the question – it was so awakening for me. It was the first time someone had asked in a way that seemed like another option was available. My mind got curious about that.

What do you see that I don't see? I wondered to myself.

In that moment I got a sense of possibility that no one had been able to point me to before. I was becoming unstuck.

A question can move us from feeling helpless to empowered, from stuck to free.

This was the start of actualising the next level of leadership in my life, by no longer being willing to tolerate certain behaviours from others or myself. I had been doing a shoddy job of trying to formulate my needs into powerful asks, and I had been doing an even shoddier job of setting boundaries and standards. The standards we allow are the standards we get. I wanted to create this 'not tolerating' from an energy of love, not an energy of fear. I had some work to do.

This marked the start of some deep coaching work. There were a lot of tears, pain, hurt and anger. Those emotions all began to surface. My healing had begun. This wasn't therapy – it was creating. I hadn't been broken and I didn't need fixing. This wasn't about changing the behaviour of others – this was focused on changing me. Changing how I saw myself, changing how I was playing the game. Starting with decision-making. This was about backing myself, and showing myself that I was strong enough to deal with any fallout. The cost of indecision and inaction had become far costlier than the consequences of taking the decision and seeing it through. All of my power had been leaked for so long by focusing on growing another person resistant to growth, instead of focusing on growing me. Now it was time to realise *my* potential.

What makes a question carry so much gravitas?

Quite simply – presence. While you are on your unique curriculum and will have your own power-hitting questions, what they will be is unknown in advance. I do know the highest quality questions come from a stillness within, a stillness that is undisturbed by the voice of the ego. A clarity of mind that we only access when we drop into presence. It can happen in a millisecond – and it can happen at any moment.

In my case, the right question came from the presence of my coach and his ability to stay with me and hear what I needed, beyond what I was saying I wanted. It was the work he had done on himself that allowed him to be an unconditionally loving champion for me, with no focus on himself. It was his profound listening that created the perfect question for me at that moment.

The question also worked because of my willingness to face where I was not expressing and living from my higher self. I was listing my insecurities and fears without using them as a weapon against myself. I wasn't judging my judgements, and he wasn't judging my story. All of these factors provided the space for high-quality questions to emerge.

The next stage of my healing and growth work was served by another high-quality question: 'When you are afraid of losing that, what would you love to keep or gain?'

I listed everything I wanted to create, plus all the insecurities, fears and doubts that might hinder this. I listed where I wanted something and thought it was impossible, and I owned where I couldn't see a way. Then I looked again for a deeper truth.

You might be starting to see a theme here. It's about moving out of loss and into gain; out of fear and into power. Out of victim and into creator. Shedding the old false identities and inviting in the deeper truth. Dropping out of the noise of the personal mind and allowing wisdom to come through. First the release, and then the creation.

The double-edged sword of strengths

This experience was here to show me parts of myself that needed to step up: my leadership and my view of myself. I woke up to where I had been ignoring my deeper knowing, a knowing that had been knocking on the door and telling me to take action. Yet until now, I had kept the door closed and opted for *business as usual*.

Why did I not take action at the time? Why was I tolerating so much for so long? Because of what I call the *double-edged sword of strengths*. My coach's question had me notice that my gift in one area – as a team player, developing, nurturing, supporting and encouraging others – was costing the greater mission. That very gift was causing a blind spot in me. I was supporting the slowest hiker to climb the mountain when the safety of the group required me to escort her off the mountain and put together a high-performing team. It hadn't even occurred to me the other option was available.

I had learned a way of doing things that was no longer serving me. I began to realise that the way of being which had got me this far in life was not going to get me to the next level.

Being open to change

These insights landed in me in a way that made a profound difference in my life. A few years earlier, they might not have had the same effect. Why? Because I wouldn't have heard them in the same way. We often think that we are open until something triggers us and all our old feelings and patterns whoosh in. Our old behaviours and our need to be right take control. The changes I am pointing to here and the results you hear me mention come from being willing to do some of the hardest, most challenging inner work I have ever done. That's why we talk about tolerating truth as a symbol of your strength. Over the past seven years, I have been learning to listen differently. I have been softening and opening. I have been practising letting go and not taking things personally. I have been letting go of the need to be right. I have been doing all of this daily, and in the development of that internal landscape, I have primed myself ready for insight.

I encourage you to stay open, to learn to let go, to allow your mind to rest in curiosity – curiosity for a different possibility. Even if you don't yet believe something to be possible, be willing to consider it *could* be.

Imagine you are trying to climb over a wall. You've tried everything you can think of, but you can't find a way to get over it. Then someone comes along and says, 'You know about the door, right?' At that moment, your mind drops into possibility – *What? What door?* Suddenly a different result seems possible. Even if you don't yet know there is actually a door there, you have just been opened up to the idea that there might be. It has become a possibility. *That* is the kind of openness we are looking to develop.

Prime your internal environment and put your high-quality questions to the wisdom of the white space, not the dot. Ask, and then let the white space do the heavy lifting. We don't get the answers from hard, forced thinking, from overworking the dot. We get the answers from a relaxed mind. Ask it what you want guidance on, then allow the answer to come to you. Plant high-quality seeds with high-quality questions for yourself, and you will reap a rich harvest!

ACTIVITY: Exploring the white space

Think about an area in life where you want something. It needs to be something that is within your influence. For example, I want to forgive, I want a relationship or *I want to be able to say no.*

Write that down and then record your responses to the following questions.

- What is the powerful question you want to be asked about this?
- What is the powerful question you *don't* want to be asked about this?

Consider other areas of your life and rerun the questions above in different contexts. Those contexts could include:

- Career
- Romantic relationships
- Social life
- Finances
- Leadership

For a curated list of twenty-five powerful questions that nourish the mind, head over to your book's bonus resources, available for you at https://trulyyoubook.com/resources.

Key insights

- Questions are instructions for the mind. Choose how you are instructing yours. High-quality questions expand your thinking and unlock fresh insights. Low-grade questions create low-grade thinking, leading to overwhelm, frustration and stagnation.

- A well-placed question can move us from distress to calm, and from stuck to free by inviting us into different perspectives and mindsets.

- We don't have to wait for someone else to provide the question. We can learn to upgrade the quality of our self-talk by asking ourselves higher-quality questions that transform our emotional state. Think creator, not victim mindset.

- Our go-to strengths can unknowingly limit our growth and progression. Becoming conscious of this double-edged sword can help us to diversify our approach and expand far beyond our current results.

- Questions are a catalyst for change; however, the answers might not be coming because we don't *think* it is possible. Stay open, get still and drop into presence – the wisdom of the white space will provide both the question and the answers.

Lesson 12
Allow Everything, Accommodate Little

You might remember in Part One where I introduced you to a few people – Amanda's partner who kept leaving the dishes in the sink, and the guy whose socks couldn't seem to find the laundry basket. I promised you back then that I was pointing you to a position of empowerment, not a lifetime of cleaning up after people! And here it is. The distinction illustrates how we can respond to unwanted behaviours while being rooted in love. If you know you have some people-pleasing tendencies, listen up. This one is especially relevant for you. We're going to talk about healthy boundaries.

Defining unconditional love

I read somewhere that unconditional love is allowing someone to be exactly as they are *and* exactly as they are not. I had this as a screensaver on my phone for a year, and it helped me immensely come back to peace. If I was triggered by someone, I would glance at my phone and use those words as an invitation to be that way towards that person now. *Everyone is doing the best they can with the thinking they have*, I would say to myself. It wasn't always easy, but it did work well most of the time, so I prioritised that way of being over anything else my personal thinking had to say.

It worked well until it didn't. Resentment started to build up as I felt I was always the one putting up with things, going at someone else's pace, prioritising their needs and denying my own. I sometimes felt like a doormat being walked all over and not addressing the behaviour in question. Then I realised the missing piece of the puzzle: I don't have to *accommodate* this.

I had misinterpreted the phrase about allowing someone to be exactly as they are and exactly as they are not. I thought that allowing other people to be fully themselves meant accommodating their behaviour in my life. Now I see that I can unconditionally love someone and not have their behaviours in my life. I see how I don't have to accommodate *them* in my life. This is different from not wanting someone in my life because I am full of resentment, anger and judgement on who they are being. I allow them to be exactly as they are and I say no (from love) to having them in my life.

The 'allowing' part of the process, is, at its essence, acceptance of what is. When we allow, we are simply accepting what is. We are not resisting what is. We have removed the judgements from it. When we allow what is, we stay out of the suffering gap. This allowing, this acceptance, moves us into a calmer feeling. *They are how they are, and that is OK. They are how they are, and that is OK. They are how they are, and that is OK.*

You might want to practise this as a mantra, as a declaration to yourself, inviting yourself into this perspective – not forcing but inviting – safe in the knowledge that it does not mean accommodating any unwanted behaviours. It is simply allowing. The 'not accommodating' part is where we get into creation mode. If I am allowing, not accommodating, what would I love to create?

Unconditional love is not about dropping all boundaries. Love and boundaries can coexist. Sometimes the most loving thing to do is to let someone go. We have an interpretation of love that we're used to. To us, love looks and sounds a certain way, yet this interpretation is simply that – our unique interpretation of love, based on what we have been conditioned to believe love looks and sounds like.

Creating boundaries

I used to think that love meant always being there for people, always being a shoulder to cry on. As a result, I would find myself being the one who people came to, to air their complaints. I found myself surrounded by a lot of heavy energy and people who felt powerless and hard done by. I got something from being the one who people came to. It fed my ego on some level to be the rescuer, but it kept me in the cycle of attracting more of what I didn't want. It didn't feed my soul.

Do you remember Carolyn's invitations to me: 'This is your opportunity to see expansion in the face of adversity' and 'You could apologise to them'. She didn't massage my ego. She didn't offer sympathy and tell me how hard done by I was. She took a stand for my greatness. That was also love. We have an infinite amount of ways to express our love. This is not about black-and-white thinking, this is not about doing the opposite of what you have been doing. It is about learning to create from different thinking to what we have been used to up until now. Carolyn loved me, *and* her way of being was forming a filter. Her way of *being* attracts people ready to take ownership of their lives. It filters out those simply looking for sympathy and to complain. We don't get what we want, we get who we're being.

Boundaries can be a powerful no from a place of love because we are saying a powerful yes to something else.

I can be generous *because* of my boundaries. I often get requests from people for help, direct to my inbox. I'm not talking about requests from paying clients but about ad hoc requests for personalised, one-to-one support. I would be exhausted and burned out if I took all those on and replied to them with the level of love and support I serve with. I say no with grace because I need to yes to staying well, grounded and alert for my paying clients.

I have said things like this: *I would love to help, and I don't offer personalised one-to-one messaging like this outside of client programmes. If you share your question in the free community group that I run, I will reply in there so it can serve the community.* Some respond positively to this, while others don't. Some people get the hump and leave and talk badly about me! I don't let that bother me, though. All that is at play is what I am pointing to in this book: thoughts, feelings and behaviours. This situation isn't personal, even if it can feel like it is. It is simply the human operating system at work, together with a whole load of unquestioned thoughts, assumptions and beliefs.

I can love those people exactly as they are, even if they are speaking ill of me. I can wish for them to get help with the thoughts that are knocking them out of heaven. What they think of me is not my business. That last sentence is written from love, freedom and wholeness, not from defensiveness or aggressiveness or insecurities. The energy it comes from makes all the difference.

Navigating boundaries

It doesn't always feel easy to be boundaried, though, because – guess what – it isn't only other people that will have thinking about it. We have thinking about it too! Thinking that creates feelings like guilt. We might have been conditioned to believe that kindness means saying yes and that love means prioritising everyone but ourselves, so we will have judgements arise in our minds when we go to implement boundaries. Remember, you are only one thought away from a different experience.

Each new moment is a new opportunity to practise falling out of your intellect and into a new reservoir of creative life energy that knows exactly how to set boundaries from love, not fear. A life energy that is safe and whole.

It is so much easier to create from love when we know we are safe. I'm not talking about physical safety here – this is referring to an internal construct. It's at a spiritual level, where your soul is safe.

For example, at a professional event once, a guy I didn't know approached me. He told me he thought I should wear a dress the next day because I looked like I had great legs. I didn't know what to say. I immediately felt myself move away from internal safety, my thinking swooping in.

How dare he, I thought. *Why do men think it is OK to come up to a woman and make everything sexual?* I laughed and shrugged his comment off, making an excuse to leave the area he was in. We still had a week together at this event, though, and I wanted to be able to meet these kinds of situations from a more empowered stance.

I thought about what I would love to create here. If I was allowing him to be exactly as he was and exactly as he wasn't, *and* not accommodating this kind of remark, what would I love to do if he were to make more remarks?

First (and this is important), I connected to the deeper truth within me: *I am safe*. I connected to that part of me by questioning the automated thinking that had been triggered.

Then I practised my answer because I sensed he was going to make more remarks throughout the week-long programme. I practised saying out loud whatever occurred to me.

Thank you, but I won't be doing that, and it is not OK for you to make these remarks. Why do you think it is OK to comment on a woman's body and tell her what to wear? Whoops, I was being unsafe again. There was an aggressive, assertive tone to my voice, which was coming from fear. I was disconnected from my power.

I reconnected and tried again.

You know, why don't you wear a dress tomorrow and we can compare legs? Nope – my ego mind had swooped back in and taken the reins. Now I'd accessed a sarcastic, passive-aggressive and even, weirdly, slightly flirtatious tone.

I reconnected again. This time I nailed it.

You know, I'm a no to wearing a dress on demand and talking about my body, but I am open to a professional conversation. If you want to talk about the last exercise we just did, we can do that for five minutes.

This last reaction came from a place where I was connected to my wholeness and my safety. The energy moving through me and therefore the tone and expression were completely different. Guess what – he came up to me first thing the next day and made an unwanted remark. I allowed and didn't accommodate, just like I had practised. There were no more unwanted remarks from that moment on and by the end of the week, we swapped details and stayed in touch.

ACTIVITY: Boundaries from love

Answer the following questions, noting them in your journal or workbook:

- Where is there an opportunity in your world to practise allowing but not accommodating?
- What are the consequences of continuing to accommodate in that situation?
- What else are you missing out on when you accommodate?
- What will you commit to prioritising, so you can say no from a place of love?

I highly recommend practising speaking this aloud. Find a trusted partner and ask if they will role play with you while you get used to speaking out your boundaries and saying no from love. Just like I did – try on multiple different ways of saying the same thing.

Key insights

- Unconditional love can coexist alongside boundaries. Allowing someone to be exactly as they are, and exactly as they are not, is not about accommodating all behaviour. We can show respect for ourselves while also honouring the individuality of others.

- We can love someone exactly as they are, knowing they are doing the best they can with the thinking they have, while simultaneously letting them go because we are no longer willing to tolerate their behaviours.

- Setting and holding boundaries may stir up feelings such as guilt or anger, in others and yourself. These are uncomfortable for the ego mind. This is a result of our conditioning and what we have learned to believe acts of kindness and love look like. Recognising that these feelings are simply old, unquestioned thought patterns playing out, allows us to set and honour boundaries from a place of love, not defensiveness, resentment and fear.

- Some people will not enjoy or respect your new boundaries. This is simply a reflection of their thinking, creating their reality at that moment. It is not personal.

- A secondary gain may be keeping you from setting and honouring your boundaries.

Explore what you might be gaining by not implementing them. For example, the ego loves being the hero/rescuer.

- Your way of being can set boundaries for you. How you show up will automatically filter people in and out.

- Setting boundaries allows us to be more generous, not less. Each no is a vote for a deeper yes to something else. Honouring our own needs preserves our resources and strengthens our capacity to serve generously in meaningful ways. We cannot pour from an empty cup.

- Emotional safety can be cultivated from within by questioning the thought that triggered a fear response, going beyond the personal mind into a deeper presence and remaining open with the question 'What would I love to create?'

- Setting and maintaining our boundaries can require practice. Ask a trusted friend to role play with you as you learn to speak out your boundaries from love and wholeness. This allows you to be a powerful, graceful stance in even the most challenging interactions.

Lesson 13
The Six-Year-Old In The Boardroom Of Your Life

It can be fascinating to look back and notice how young we were when we made some of our life-defining choices: decisions around education, careers and relationships; decisions around what keeps us safe and what makes us happy; decisions around who we are, what is possible and what is not possible. Those younger versions of ourselves were innocently setting the best direction they could for our lives today from the level of awareness they had at the time. An awareness shaped by the words they heard, the patterns they saw in the world around them and the beliefs and experiences they absorbed along the way.

We think that our adult selves are making our decisions today because that is who we see looking back at us in the mirror. What if that isn't what is happening after all? What if there is a much younger version of you in the boardroom of your life still calling the shots?

An outdated view of ourselves

As we've grown up, life has evolved; the world has evolved; culture and technology have evolved. Many of us, though, continue living out decisions in our thirties, forties and fifties that we made when we were much younger, but what if those choices aren't in alignment for us now? We don't have to live our lives today according to the decisions we made in the past – decisions made based on the level of awareness we had back then. We can make new choices at any time that could move us into a life more aligned with who we are now and the contribution we want to make. Yet many of us don't feel the truth of that option to choose again. Many of us feel stuck. Why is that?

While it might be obvious in theory that we can make another choice, it does not always seem possible in reality. Thoughts swoop in about what we have to give up, what we have to let go of, fear around losing money, getting hurt, hurting others, compromising our lifestyle, and starting again. We start to feel the weight of the potential consequences, and the idea of change can suddenly seem overwhelming.

The consequences of both change and staying still

Let's not deny that there might be consequences. The cause-and-effect principle tells us that every action (cause) creates a corresponding result (effect). This isn't about trying to convince ourselves something won't happen. We can honour that part of ourselves that is concerned about the consequences. How do we honour it? With an invitation – an invitation *to explore and choose* whether the potential consequences are worth the shift. An invitation *to weigh up* the probability of them coming true. An invitation *to step into your power* by asking yourself a higher-quality question:

If those consequences did come true, what would I do then? How could I respond? What might I create or choose next?

It is so important to bring in these types of questions. Otherwise, we get lost in the idea of any unwanted effects being permanent, and can easily fall back into victim thinking in these moments. These questions invite us back into our true selves – into our power and creator perspective. From there we realise that most things are not as permanent or unchangeable as our minds might have us believe. From there, we remain open to the flow of life.

The fear of the unknown, or making a *'wrong'* choice can be so intimidating to us that we don't tend to consider how playing it safe and/or staying still could be the biggest risk of all. If you don't believe there are costs and consequences to doing nothing, pick up a tin of beans and hold it out with your arm stretched out beside you. Don't change a thing. See how much heavier it gets one hour from now, five hours from now. That's the cost of not letting it go. Doing nothing feels like the safe option, but it isn't necessarily safer – it is just more familiar. We can feel the illusion of safety from the familiar, but it is just that: an illusion.

Rewiring for success

Our brains are (thankfully) designed to keep us safe, but the brain cannot tell the difference between life-threatening danger and imagined danger.

For example, when I was living in Lake Louise, Canada, I lived in grizzly bear territory. Late one night when I was heading to my accommodation, I suddenly found myself frozen to the spot in terror. A bear, just a little ahead of me, was staring at me, and I was not carrying my bear spray. Holy shit – how do you respond to different bear attacks again? Play dead? Stand your ground? Fight back? I was trying to recap everything Parcs Canada had told us about what to do in the event of an attack.

Turns out it was a rock, not a bear. The same rock that I walked past every day. A rock that my brain had completely forgotten about when it decided there was a bear. The terror I felt was real! (Thank you for the alert brain.) The bear was not.

The point of my story is that given we are wired for safety, we can often find ourselves focusing on bears instead of rocks. In real terms, this might sound something like *What if it goes wrong?* Our minds rarely offer up *What if it goes right?*

What if it can only ever go right?

To live from a place of possibility and freedom to choose is so helpful to create a new relationship with our minds. To rewire our neural pathways to notice opportunity, beauty and blessings. You can rewire it by asking it higher-quality questions, challenging your judgements and assumptions with loving curiosity and allowing a deeper truth to come through.

What you focus on grows. If you want to see bears everywhere, you will. If you want to see rocks, get present, they are already all around you. This book and its activities are already supporting you into more presence, inviting you to get more accurate, to go beyond the stories of the ego mind and to help you rewire your mind so that you can trust and co-create with life's natural flow.

What successful people know

We sometimes get stuck in indecision or stop ourselves from making a new choice because we want to be certain that it will work out well first. What exactly is *working out well*, though? It is whatever our thoughts make up at the time. We make up the criteria, and then we place ourselves at the mercy of them.

One common trait of successful entrepreneurs and leaders is that they know *failure* is only temporary.

They also know it is not their identity. They made a choice, they took a risk, and this time it didn't pay off as they had hoped. It didn't *'work out well'*. At least, that's how it looks right now, and they understand that they can't know for sure that it hasn't worked well. They know that when one door closes, another opens. They know it could be a redirection to something even better.

In business and life, we're bound to make choices that don't turn out how we hoped. We might make investments that lose us money, we might bring people into our circles who weren't the right fit. Don't make these outcomes your identity. These are experiences, not definitions of who you are. The more someone believes that a string of failures is their identity, the more they have moved away from the truth of who they are. What if these moments are here to help you grow? Like a phoenix rising, what if these moments are here to remind you exactly who you are?

What would you choose if you knew you were fully supported by life?

The power of choice

If it feels impossible for you to choose to change, there is still a way to access a more peaceful state of mind with your current life. You can see that there is still a choice occurring. For example, you are *choosing to stay* rather than feeling like you can't leave. You could leave, but you prefer to stay than risk the consequences of making the change.

My role here is to connect you back to your power, and recognising that you are still making a choice can help you to do that. As Austrian psychologist, Viktor E Frankl said, 'Everything can be taken from a man but one thing: the last of the human freedoms, to choose one's attitude in any given set of circumstances, to choose one's own way.'[10]

Years ago, I decided to choose my attitude with my relationship to money. I made a promise to myself that I would never again say the words *I can't afford*. I started using different language, for example:

- I choose not to spend on that.
- I choose to be debt-free.
- I choose to take ownership of my financial freedom.

I also chose to become a person who can afford it. It was an invitation to myself to be different – to think and create like a financially wealthy woman. This has been a game-changer for me. It is such a different feeling and experience to live into the statement *I choose not to spend on that* rather than *I can't afford*, and to learn to think like those who have what I want and who have created wealth in ways that inspire me.

If you want to work on your relationship with money, start by trying these perspectives (or similar) for yourself for the next thirty days. Commit to feeling fully willing to believe a new perspective, as much if

---

10   VE Frankl, *Man's Search for Meaning* (Beacon Press, 2006)

not more than the current belief *that is limiting you*. Over time, you'll start to feel the energy shift. It's OK if that doesn't happen as quickly as you'd like – it can take some practice. The mind can be stubborn, and the ego is a playful trickster with an amazing advertising department! It can get us to believe our current thinking so much that it can seem hard to feel the truth in another way of thinking.

How does our younger self impact our current life subconsciously?

I was brought up listening to words and phrases like *'It's rude to stare'*. I was taught from a young age not to look at strangers and not to make eye contact. I learned that to keep myself safe, the strategy was *head down; don't look up; don't get their attention*. It was all about contraction – about being small, about making myself invisible – and it generally seemed to work.

The problem is, I still do it. I'm not a small child anymore, and not everyone and every situation is dangerous, but I catch myself walking around avoiding eye contact.

This pattern of contraction plays out in different areas of my life and a common frustration of mine is not being truly seen and understood. Can you spot the irony of being taught it is safe to not stand out and then feel the pain of not being seen?

For example, in non-dangerous situations as an adult, I used to choose to sit at the back of the room whenever

I attended events. I would never put my hand up to ask a question in a group setting. I would wait to be spoken to instead of approaching first and asking if someone would like some company. What the heck? I love people, I love being in conversation, I love learning, so why am I acting all small and funky about this? Because my innocent little inner child is in the director's seat and I am unconscious of what is going on.

Throughout our lives, from an early age, we make many subconscious choices. These might include the choice not to be embarrassed, the choice not to get it wrong, the choice not to get rejected, the choice that you are not worthy and the choice to not get hurt. These are choices we don't realise we are making. We also don't realise these choices have formed habits that now operate on autopilot. Now we need to wake up to them and give them an overhaul. I am pleased to report that I have cut out these particular behaviours and I now have no issue with sitting front and centre, approaching people first and speaking my question into the room!

Our current lives are a result of the unquestioned decisions and choices we have made in the past. There's so much wisdom in those choices. At the time, we were doing our best, and on some level, it made sense to make those decisions, so we can forgive that younger version of ourselves. They were doing the best they could with what they had available to them at the time. Make peace with your inner child, give them some love and reassurance so they can give up the director's chair. Now you are free to claim that seat at the table.

> **ACTIVITY: Reclaiming your boardroom**
>
> Grab your notebook again and make notes on the following points.
>
> - What decision from your past no longer feels aligned with who you are today? Notice anything that feels ready to be reimagined.
> - How do you sense your younger self is directing your current life?
>
> Now identify the memory of where you made this choice and complete the sentence: I chose at the age of _____ to _____. Take a moment to acknowledge the decisions of your younger self. They were doing their best for you at the time.
>
> - What do you now need to release to make space for alignment and growth?
>
> Finally, fill in the gap in this sentence: Today I choose to _____ in service of my wildest dreams and in service of my next-level life.

Key insights

- Reclaim the director's chair! Many of the choices playing out in our lives today have been shaped by a younger version of ourselves.

- We continue to act out these old choices because they bring a sense of the familiar. Holding on to familiar but outdated decisions, habits and behaviours creates an illusion of safety that stagnates growth.

- Our brains are wired for safety, but they cannot tell the difference between real and imaginary danger. Questioning our assumptions alongside cultivating a deeper sense of self empowers us to make new choices rooted in possibility and not in fear.

- We always have the power to choose our attitude. Owning our choices shifts us from feeling restricted to a sense of empowerment. There is a significant difference between 'I am choosing to stay' vs 'I cannot leave'.

- By recognising the role of the inner child in our choices, and that they were doing the best they could from the viewpoint they had, we can thank them for the part they played until now. Reassure them and realign our choices with who we are today, minus any self-judgement or blame.

So there you have it: thirteen lessons to take with you into the next chapter of your life, a chapter that can be created in alignment with your highest self, if you're willing to get on the court, and follow its call.

Living from a connection to your inner leadership, you will create paradigm shifts for your life and the lives of those you love.

This kind of leadership:

- Is played on the court
- Looks through the lens of the creator

- Forgives and releases judgement
- Honours its word
- Asks the higher-quality questions
- Recognises the freedom to make new choices
- Creates boundaries from love
- Positions the higher self in the director's seat

What might that kind of leadership create? What becomes possible when you play the game that way?

Coming up next are five powerful invitations to help you embrace that kind of leadership fully. Let's design your Life 2.0!

PART THREE
AN INVITATION TO YOUR LIFE 2.0

An Invitation To...

Be Your Future Self Now

I magine walking around in a dark room all your life, and then realising one day that there is a light switch. You hit the switch, and the room is illuminated instantly. No more fumbling around in the dark – you now see clearly. You realise that you never have to go back to being in the dark.

Imagine you have driven the 10-mile trip to work every day for the last five years. Then one day, you get a lift with a friend, and they take a shortcut you never knew existed. You don't have to continue driving the long way around now you know about the shortcut. The shortcut is available for you to take now.

Imagine you have a new understanding. An understanding of inside-out living. An understanding that you are only one thought away from a different experience and that when you drop out of the personal mind into the stillness within, new ideas, solutions, fresh thought and infinite creativity can come through. An understanding that you are not your thoughts, you are not your feelings, you are not your conditioning, you are not your past and your identity is not fixed. Well, guess what – you don't have to imagine, because that understanding is available to you now. A deeper truth of who you are is available to you now.

After spending time with this book, reflecting on the lessons and completing the activities, you will start to see the availability of the light switch for your life. Just like the patient who went from distressed to still in an instant, you don't have to gradually turn up the light. It isn't a dimmer switch. It is an on-off switch, and you can set it to on.

Shifting our mindset

We know now that if we can use thought to create suffering, we can also use it in the other direction, to dream, to expand our sense of what is possible and to create momentum. We can use the gift of thought for us, to uplift and energise, and to serve our highest good.

Using your gift in this way is the next step to creating a more aligned and fulfilling life. Ask yourself higher-quality questions and plant the seeds in the white space to let it know you'd like support identifying the answers. What is it that you want for your life?

I've provided some questions that I love to sit with to evoke insights. Spend time with the ones that you are drawn to – you don't have to answer them all. They will help you start to consider the next chapter of your life:

What am I being called to create?

One year from now, what would I love to be saying about my life?

What are the values I want to live by for this next year?

What contribution do I want to make?

What would be fun?

Who and what is important to me in this season of my life?

What do I really care about?

If I knew I couldn't fail, what would I make a priority?

What will I say no to this year?

What would I love to say yes to this year?

What do I want my legacy to be?

What would make this season of my life meaningful?

The next part involves upgrading our listening. This requires bringing conscious awareness to how we are relating to our self-talk. Practise releasing limitations by dropping the resistance and judgement.

Practise getting still inside by going beyond the personal mind. This way we can listen and connect to a greater voice already within. We want to tune in to a higher frequency and *allow* ourselves to be moved into action by what we hear coming through. We can practise this now, with these questions, and we can practise developing our listening in our everyday life, with everyday moments. It is a constant, consistent practice that will serve your growth well.

'Allow' is the keyword here. For me, it seems like allowing is the way I would describe how I live my life. It might sound odd, and it hasn't always been how I would describe things, but that seems to be the way it is these days – an allowing of the higher self, which I am calling *Poppet*, to be expressed, like something else has taken the remote control and I am simply following orders. At times, the ego doesn't want to follow *Poppet's* orders. At times, following *Poppet's* orders doesn't appear to make any logical sense. Sometimes what I think I want and what *Poppet* wants for me don't seem to be on the same page at all – and I say this with a smile on my face because underneath all that, there is a lightness, and a peace knowing that *Poppet* is always on the right page. When I insist that I am, and she is not, ploughing ahead with forcing things to be the way I think they should be, she has infinite ways of nudging me back on track. Some of her ways are more comfortable than others. Some are more of a wallop than a nudge. I have grown to see that I quite like delegating decisions anyway, so relaxing into trusting that *Poppet* knows what she is doing, works great for me, and I can stop forcing, resisting and trying so hard.

How does *Poppet* come through? I tend to have a sense of something, a feeling for something, you might know it as intuition, a gut sense. Others are more auditory and more visual. You do you, I simply write in this way as this is how I experience it. I take the orders through a feeling like I shared with you in my health scare story, and before I know it, I am moved into action – not from force but from a power moving through me. That power is *Poppet*. It is all about learning to listen to ourselves differently.

Allowing doesn't make us passive. This approach makes us active participants in this game of life, very much so. Our role is to get still and listen, and then the answers appear. When they do, we have our direction of travel. We have our vision for the next chapter. Now we serve that vision.

We can serve it now because we can be different now, not tomorrow, not someday. We think we have been doing our best up until now, and we have, but that best was from an outdated view of ourselves. We were simply operating in alignment with beliefs that we thought were our personalities, identities and ceilings, limiting the possibility and results. I was watching a show on TV here in the UK, where two families swapped lives. One was poor and one was rich. (Their words, not mine.) The poor family had a view (an assumption) that something wasn't possible for them because they didn't have the money to invest to get started. The rich family shared with them a way that they could get started without needing any capital. The only thing that stood in the way was that the poor family didn't *think* it was possible, so they didn't bother to find out if there was a way. As soon as they got a sniff that there was, they stepped into action.

Now we have woken up to a deeper truth of who we are, we don't need to keep wearing the out-of-date clothes that don't fit or align with this truth. It is time to step into better-fitting gear. It is time to embrace and embody the one who has already lived your next-level life. It is time to *be your future you!*

Stepping into our future self

Our subconscious mind does not know the difference between real news and fake news. It is why people with a fear of spiders can have a panic attack at the mention of a spider, even if there is no spider in the room. Their mind thinks and believes there is. The thought is enough to trigger a physiological response.

It is why Olympic athletes use visualisation as part of their training programmes. The athletes are mentally running the race in their mind, over and over, visualising it and adding emotional charge. It isn't a passive attraction – this is a being and a doing. Visualisation activates the motor cortex, the part of the brain that sends signals to activate movement in the body.

When we know the power of these kinds of approaches, we can use them to our advantage.

Start to live as your future state *now*. You don't have to wait for your circumstances to change for you to change. If you notice yourself saying things like 'I don't know what I want, the answers aren't coming, my vision isn't clear', then put *those challenges* to your future self. How did my future self approach this? What did they do to get clear? Your future self is full of wisdom and will have some high-quality questions and answers for you. They have already overcome this challenge.

You might find it helpful to shift to a different part of the room and imagine it is one year from now or five years from now. You are looking back to where you were sitting a moment ago, looking back at your current day self with so much love and compassion and encouragement for them. Observe them. What advice do you have for them from here – from the place where you now stand – from the position in the future where you have already overcome the challenge they are sitting with?

Keep imagining the you in one, five, ten years from now. How do they show up? What habits do you notice? What are they no longer spending their time on? What rooms are they in? What contributions have they made? What do they earn? How are they interacting with themselves, with others, with opportunities? How are they creating their opportunities? Notice them. Start to think like them. The capacity to do that is already within you. Go there in your mind. Imagine it. Visualise it. Feel into it.

For many years now, I have been doing just that. Every morning I connect to my living vision

– a document that has without a shadow of a doubt helped me transform my wildest dreams into reality. It is a heart-led invitation into a way of being in my life. It is my compass point for how I live each day. It is a reminder to connect me back to truth. It is a rocket up my ass at times when I forget who I am and need a bit of a loving nudge into action. My document is upgraded each year. It is always evolving as I evolve, and the shifts that have occurred in my life as a result of my commitment to following this north star are amazing.

Elevated-being states and actions create elevated results. Your future is created from the present moment. The present is all we ever have to work with. Let's open our hearts and our minds, and let's get to work! It is time to create your own living vision.

Head over to the activity, make yourself comfortable and have fun with it. This is an act of love, an act of creation, an act of service for your life. How would your future self approach it? Be that now.

ACTIVITY: One year from now – your living vision

Imagine the date is one year from now and we bump into each other in the street. You come over to me and say, 'Lisa, reading your book was life-changing for me. This year I have...'

Now capture what comes up.

Tips: Make sure it is at least 50% doable and includes both external and internal shifts, eg What do you have? Who are you being? How do you feel? Who do you spend time with? Write from the heart.

Read what you have written out loud as though it has truly happened. Allow your heart to connect to the aliveness of this for you. Then, from that connection to your future state, look back at yourself today.

Give yourself some advice and words of encouragement as to how you lived each day that created those results. Embodying the future state, embodying the you who has already lived that year and created all of this: What do they have to offer you? What are they telling you to do? Now go do it!

Keep it visible, take a picture of it and have it as your screensaver on your phone, or print it out and read it every morning. Imagine stepping into the paper. Imagine stepping into the version of you that created it, and then be that now!

Many, many, many people won't do this. They will rush ahead, read the next thing or think that sounds like a good idea without actually doing it.

Remember the regrets of the dying. Print your words out. Keep them visible. Every day. Breathe life into what you have written, and have it breathe life into you. This becomes your instruction manual for playing the game.

After one week of living this way, reflect: What opportunities and insights have come up from living this way? What do you want to adjust in how you are showing up? Then rinse, and repeat! Consistency of living from our highest self is key.

An Invitation To...

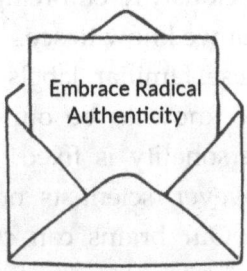

There are lots of things to look out for when we're shooting for transformational change. One trick the ego mind loves is convincing us that the familiar is authentic and that the unfamiliar is inauthentic. We're wiser than that, though! Read on to learn more so you don't fall for your ego mind's cheeky games.

Stepping out of the familiar

I'm shy. I'm an introvert. I'm too proud. I'm not like that. I don't think that way...

Labels. Our minds love to label and compartmentalise. The brain receives a phenomenal amount of information through our senses every second. So it does what it can to preserve energy, it will delete, distort and generalise the information it is receiving. Which means it is automatically filtering information in and out, according to how we see the world. We're therefore subconsciously re-enforcing what is familiar to us. We see what we know to see.

Over time these familiar labels about ourselves become what we know to be our personality, and we think our personality is fixed. At one point so did science. However, scientists now acknowledge that is not true. Our brains can continue to learn and to be rewired and reprogrammed way beyond our childhood.[11] Which means that we can reinvent ourselves whenever we choose. How cool is that?

At school, I didn't know that, though. I thought I was my personality. I thought that if you acted in alignment with your personality, that was called authenticity, not realising it was simply familiar.

CASE STUDY: Playing it safe

As an August baby in the English school system, I was always one of the youngest in my year. I had been taught to respect my elders, and I had learned from a

---

11 M Frankel, 'How to alter your personality: why your character isn't fixed in stone', *New Scientist* (12 January 2022), www.newscientist.com/article/mg25333690-900-how-to-alter-your-personality-why-your-character-isnt-fixed-in-stone, accessed 8 October 2024

young age that I was shy. I was told it was better to be quiet, stay safe and do as I was told, and I was taught to be polite and respectful.

I lived in jeans and T-shirts. Whenever I wore a skirt or a dress, people would make an exaggerated *Wooooooo* noise when they saw me. 'Wooooooo, she's got legs!' people would say, which drove me mad.

Because I was wired to believe it was better to go unnoticed, I did what I needed to get the attention off me, to stop the embarrassment of being in the spotlight. I stropped upstairs to my room to change back into my jeans and T-shirt and then remained in a grump with the people who had just made it impossible for me to wear a skirt. So that's it then, at the age of eleven. Who I am now, is who I am. That will dictate how I behave and what I can and cannot have, and that is the end of the matter.

When I look back now, I think I sensed that I wasn't living my truth. I knew when it felt I was out of alignment with who I was underneath all this conditioning and labelling. I came alive on the sports field and within my close circle of friends, but I played a smaller and meeker version of myself outside of those scenarios.

I believed I couldn't just come back after the school holidays and suddenly be a different person. A more extroverted person. A more visible, vocal person. A skirt wearer instead of a trouser wearer. Nope – I was a good kid with decent grades who liked sports and art, who had a small group of nice friends and wore trousers. That was me. That was familiar. That was Lisa.

Don't get me wrong – I am so blessed for my childhood – this isn't a message about lack. This is about me mistaking familiar for truth and authenticity.

I've seen the power available in knowing that familiar is not necessarily authentic. At mid-life I have reinvented myself many times over. These days it is a daily – heck, a moment-by-moment – occurrence, and it can be so fun!

Change is always available to us, and yet we consistently fall into the familiarity trap.

Why we accept our labels

We innocently cling to the known, to the patterns and behaviours that have shaped our lives until now. We mistake those for the essence of who we are. We miss that this familiarity is an internal construct. This construct is not our true nature – it is something we've unconsciously adopted. We have believed our labels and let them go on without questioning. We then recreate familiar scenarios, which reinforce our made-up sense of identity, even when that identity no longer serves us. Even worse, we don't just recreate the scenarios, we *fight* for them. We fight for our smallness. We fight to keep the scenarios alive. This is the work of the ego, not our true self.

A friend shared with me once that she had feelings for someone who she wanted to get to know better. I asked her what she was going to do about it. She said to me, 'Nothing, he has to ask me, I am too proud to make the first move!' Can you see how it shows up – *I am too proud* to make the first move! Familiar – not authentic.

Imagine going to the cinema to watch a movie, in which aliens have landed and are taking over the world. When the movie finishes, you don't leave the cinema because you're afraid if you go outside you'll be gobbled up by the aliens. Forgetting it's a movie and acting as though it's real would be ridiculous, right? That's what we do with labels. That's what we do with things that feel familiar. We forget they are labels, we have got so used to wearing them.

Time to switch it up

To mistake the familiar for authentic is to deny the expression of our dynamic, ever-evolving nature – the creative life force that runs through us – our actual authentic self. I encourage you to learn to distinguish between the two. This will require a conscious effort to question your feelings, understand the origins of your feelings and recognise when they are keeping you tethered to a version of yourself that no longer exists.

> Labels are layers that can be peeled off. They are not permanent identities.

Familiar might feel like the safer choice, but how safe will it feel to look back on your life with no more time to make changes and regret that you hadn't owned your truth in the moments when you had time to do something about it? Instead of believing your familiar feelings are authentic, step into courage, step into curiosity, and bring a willingness to live beyond the confines of what feels familiar. You've got this!

ACTIVITY: Cutting out labels

Pick a familiar, limiting label you have been wearing.

Reflect on where that label came from. Whose voice are you still carrying?

What are you afraid will happen if you don't believe this label?

One truth about me that this label hides is...

Close your eyes and imagine yourself without this label.

Who are you without this label? What qualities emerge now? What new freedom have you accessed now you no longer carry that label?

What is one high-impact action you can take that will be guided by truth rather than this label?

An Invitation To...

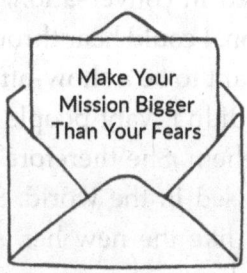

Make Your Mission Bigger Than Your Fears

Now we're starting to create a vision for our next twelve months, and we're letting go of the labels and feelings we've mistakenly been believing to be our authentic selves. Do we just feel the fear and do it anyway, or is there another way?

Overcoming barriers

Alice had a wonderful gift and a powerful vision, but there seemed to be something in the way of her owning this gift and stepping into her vision. Her talents could make a valuable meaningful contribution to many, and yet when we met, Alice would dumb her vision down and shrug it off, and come up with many reasons why she needed to focus on something else instead. There was something that stopped her from being fully expressed and of her highest service.

As we explored in conversation, I started to spot what was going on. I could hear through her language that she didn't want to be a show-off, she didn't want to brag, and she didn't want people to think that she was better than them. She therefore didn't allow her gifts to be expressed in the world. She was worried people wouldn't like the new her, she was worried she would lose clients, she was worried she would lose money and no one would want what she was now offering. Alice is not on her own. Many people have wings that they clip, so that other people don't get jealous, intimidated or upset, so that they fit in and aren't seen as different or better than others.

Some people will not enjoy seeing you shine bright, some people will feel threatened, some people will worry about being left behind, and some people will experience jealousy. Wherever there is change, some people will make it about themselves and what it means for them. It is the very nature of us humans to focus on fear and loss and to focus on ourselves. Our brains were wired that way to help keep us alive. While we are no longer hunter-gatherers, the reptilian part of our brain is still operating the out-of-date system.

Love those people anyway.

We're all doing the best we can with the thinking we are believing in any moment.

Remember what I said about allowing everything and accommodating little. Remember what I said about what you think of me is not my business. I'll say it again – if 10,000 people read this book, there will be 10,000 different versions of the same book. I know I am writing from a connected place inside of me, connected to my mission to help people shine. To support them in living their most alive life. To ease them out of their limitations and into their wellbeing, clarity of mind and powerful expression. By doing so, creating a kinder, safer world. One where people take ownership of their own judgements and assumptions and move through them, instead of projecting out and blaming others.

Whether this book lands with you is not for me to say. I know the place I came from when I wrote it. That is what has allowed me to be real, raw and vulnerable and to bring it to life and share it in the world. The mission is bigger than any fears of other people's judgements.

Now, back to Alice. For the rest of our session, we explored many reasons why sharing her gifts with the world wasn't bragging, wasn't showing off, wasn't being better than. We then explored how sharing her gifts could be an act of service, an act of love.

I asked her, 'Do you remember that body of work I shared with you?'

She said, 'Yes.'

I asked, 'What difference did it make to you?'

She told me that it offered her relief. She said it made her respond and react differently in her life with many things. She said it gave her freedom. She said that without the understanding she gained from it, there would have been many an opportunity she would have turned down. She talked about potential business that was coming her way as a result of being able to say yes to those opportunities.

She said her old way of being wouldn't have answered the door to those opportunities knocking. She told me how she would previously have had a suspicious mind, and she would have listened and acted in alignment with her self-doubt. She would have listened to her feelings and the stories they were telling her as fact and truth, and her behaviours would have been in alignment with those stories. She told me that the body of work I shared, along with the conversations we were having, had opened her up to a new understanding and a new possibility, and from this way of being, multiple opportunities have been created.

By this point, Alice was moved to tears and connected to the power of expressing our gifts and the difference they can make. She was out of her personal mind and into her heart. She was seeing how she owed it to her mission to share her talents with the world. When we come from the energy of service we come from a mission that is on purpose. Whatever your mission is, whether it is being a voice of impact, or being a role model that inspires others. When we focus our way of being to come from there, that's the place where the ego does not live. That's your pure essence. Express your gifts from there. That part of you will have no issues in sharing your gifts. That part of you desires to be in service. That part of you has no concerns about bragging. It is pure love. It is truly you. When we connect to a reason greater than ourselves, the fears and doubts shrink in comparison and we become giants. It is like Marianne Williamson said: 'Your playing small does not serve the world.'[12]

Like Alice, you get to choose what you focus on.

Shine the light on your mission

---

12 M Williamson, *A Return to Love: Reflections on the Principles of 'A Course in Miracles'* (HarperOne, 1996)

> **ACTIVITY: Mission possible**
>
> Make notes on all the following questions.
>
> - If fear wasn't holding you back, what impact – big or small – would you want to have in the world?
> - What about that is important to you?
> - Why is that important to you?
> - As you connect to your deeper *why* and the importance of your mission, what is one small courageous act you can take this week to honour it?
> - What values will you live by to honour it?
> - Is there anything you want to add to your 'living vision' that will align it more with your mission?
>
> Come back here later and reflect:
>
> - How was it, living in alignment with your mission?
> - What did you learn about yourself after taking courageous action?

A great way of staying on the path of this change journey towards a more authentic purposeful life is to pause and acknowledge the progress already made. That is in the next invitation… Come and join me!

An Invitation To...

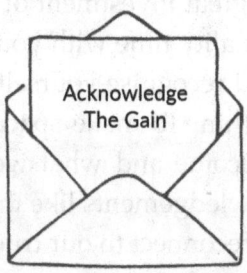

One of the processes I guide people through involves taking time to acknowledge what has been created and accomplished in their lives over the past decade. Not just on an external level, but on an internal level too. This always moves people in ways they never expected. It always ignites an internal motivation for what they might now create in their future and an expansion for what they believe is possible.

Shifting our perceptions

The view we carry about ourselves shapes how we interact with the world, so we must recognise the true capacity within us. However, we are not hardwired to notice our greatness. We don't slow down and make time and space for a deeper connection to our brilliance. It is a great investment of time and energy to spend some quality time with yourself in this way. To appreciate and recognise yourself. To really, really see the giant within. To make space for recognising who we have become and what we have achieved. Authentic acknowledgements like this can cultivate a flow state as we reconnect to our true nature.

Acknowledgements are a way of intentionally training the mind to focus. To shine the light in the direction of greatness, uniqueness, power, agency, capability and capacity. It isn't about being better than anyone. It isn't about comparison. No one needs to feel good about themselves by comparing themselves with others. No one needs to criticise anyone else to acknowledge themselves or another. Slowed-down time with acknowledgements is a way to a nicer feeling.

When we live our lives constantly moving the goalposts – constantly seeking the next thing, constantly wanting more, bigger, better – we never feel fulfilled, content or satisfied, or at least not for long. We don't feel these feelings as a way of life, as a default feeling. We mistakenly think that the outcome is what we need to feel happier, and then off we go again without spending any time recognising the accomplishment, in seeing who we really are.

We're often spending time focusing on the gap. Focusing on what we don't have yet. Thinking and believing that the next thing will bring us joy and satisfaction. It might, momentarily – or rather, your thinking about having the thing will bring you joy – until the thinking is gone. Until the thinking is replaced with more thinking that is now telling you there is something else you need to feel that joy again.

We are living in a convenience-led world, where we want to have everything instantly. In the searching and the seeking of the next thing, though, we miss out on the trip. We don't pause to take in who we are and see the beauty in this moment. We don't pause to reflect on the magic of what has already been created. We don't take any time to value and deeply appreciate and connect with who we are, what we already have and who we are becoming.

Unlocking our potential

When asked to do this acknowledgement process, people can struggle at first. The mind likes to diminish or trivialise the success, making it smaller than it was, filtering out wins by telling us they don't count or they were too easy. We have this weird idea that we have to work hard at something for it to be valuable and for it to count as a success. Ever noticed yourself doing that? *Oh, that doesn't really count, because it was easy.*

We undermine our strengths and gifts because they come naturally to us, yet these are the things that don't come naturally to others. These are your strengths and gifts, and yet here you are, diminishing them in your mind's eye instead of owning their brilliance. Acknowledging the gain is a process that has people really connect to what it took to be able to be where you are now.

Soon after the publication of this book, I will be featured in a *USA TODAY* article, 'Celebrating Exceptional Women & Men Leaders Who Are Inspiring Change'. I caught myself in conversation with someone, and I was about to play it down. Instead, I paused and connected to what went into creating it. I was the one that put myself in the rooms that got me noticed. I was the one who worked through all the limitations, fears and doubts in my personal mind. I was the one who was willing to jump before I felt ready, multiple times over. I was the one willing to be a yes to investing in myself, multiple times over. All of that and so much more is what it took to create that opportunity.

I promise to never consciously undersell myself to myself again, and when I notice that I am, I commit to coming back to honouring my greatness. Not from arrogance or from feeling better than others, but from a place of grounding and connection to my authentic self.

AN INVITATION TO... ACKNOWLEDGE THE GAIN

Sometimes people believe the myth that we need to be under pressure to feel motivated, and that focusing on what is missing somehow keeps us driven. What I would say to that is, *Sure, if that works for you.* I don't see it that way. I love creating for the joy of the creating process, and acknowledging the gain isn't about being complacent and staying where you are. This is about creating from aliveness, with aliveness. This is about enjoying the creation process from a place of love and connectedness, instead of creating from a place of need and insufficiency and a misunderstanding that your okayness and validation come from external results and accomplishments.

The more capable I see myself to be, the more I contribute to new heights. I love working towards something. I love setting lofty goals and having a legacy to build. I love having a direction to travel in and then living in the unknown of how that will all come about while getting still and simply following the nudge to create.

This book is one of those creations. I didn't set out with a goal to write a book. When I discovered coaching, I knew that my legacy was now underway, to help transform lives and help people step into their more empowered being states and live lives that they love. Why do I care about that? Because safety is a big value of mine, and I truly believe that when people feel free, uplifted and loved, they show up to life and each other differently. Hurt people do hurtful things to others, so I do care about uplifting the consciousness of humanity. It isn't all altruistic motivation – it benefits me too. I get to walk about in a safer, kinder world.

We have been given these wild and wonderful gifts – the gift of imagination, of creative thought, the gift of being able to rewire our minds, the gift of feeling love, compassion and empathy. These gifts can serve us and help create a kinder world. We have everything within us, and we simply need to let it be expressed. We can't express it if we're not connected to it. What if today you took a look back over the past decade from your life and created a timeline? What did you achieve? What did you overcome? Who did you become? What are you most proud of? What did you learn about forgiveness, strength, love, compassion? Who did you help?

ACTIVITY: Ten years of achievements

On a blank piece of paper, write down the year it was ten years ago and the age you were then. Work your way through year by year, recalling highlight moments you have taken part in and experiences you had from then until now.

What are the key moments or achievements that stand out to you over the past ten years? What have you accomplished or experienced that you are proud of? What qualities have you cultivated?

Reflect on the learning from all those moments. Connect to who you became as a result of stepping into those achievements, and into overcoming any

AN INVITATION TO... ACKNOWLEDGE THE GAIN

obstacles and curveballs. Connect to how much you have experienced.

In one or two sentences, describe the most important gain you've made in the past decade – who you are now that you weren't before.

Now, as you stay connected to the power within, write down your answers to the questions:

- What becomes possible for the next decade?
- What would make this coming decade, the best decade yet?

An Invitation To...

Make Powerful, Meaningful Commitments

A n acknowledgement of you, dear reader...
Congratulations – you have arrived at the final few pages of what I hope has been an insightful journey for you. We have covered a lot of ground and opened up some new, fresh ideas of who you are and what might be possible for you now.

If you are feeling a desire for change, for things to be different in some way – whether that be the game itself, the player or both – the final invitation I have for you here is to make some powerful commitments for yourself.

My life changes most when I commit to change. A commitment to deepening the realising of who I am. A commitment to living a life on purpose, with my whole heart and in a way that I can be proud of. A commitment to my mission. A commitment to having women's voices heard, valued and recognised. A commitment to a world where we no longer have to have the gender-equality conversation because equality exists as the norm. A commitment to creating a kinder, safer world through raising the consciousness of humanity.

I start at this level, with a vision for the mission and a connection to what matters, along with a connection to self. It is this purpose that helps me create game-line commitments. For example, if I want this to happen, one way of contributing is to get my voice out there on a larger scale, so a commitment to getting my book published becomes a priority.

People can be resistant to the word commitment. I shared an example of that from my life in the chapter on integrity, Lesson 7. Yet the word commitment is neutral. It is the personal mind that attaches the meaning to it, which causes the resistance. The truth is, we're always committing to something in any moment. We can often be committed to our fears, our hesitations and our concerns. We can be committed to our small selves.

Of course, change can feel scary, daunting and intimidating. It can feel risky. There is a lot of unknown, and that can be uncomfortable for many people. If that is you, I have an idea for you: I highly recommend making a powerful commitment to building a great friendship with discomfort!

Make your commitments

To help you create some commitments for yourself, I want to share with you a few things that have been really helpful for me.

1. Connect to your deepest why

What do you want to create? What do you want to stand for? What is important about this for you?

When we can get really connected to the things that truly matter, it can help ignite within us a deeper commitment to keep going and create sustainable change. You can see in this book some of the things that I care deeply about, which make me show up even when I don't feel like it. If you haven't done the activity in the earlier invitation to make your mission bigger than your fears, go and do it. This will help you find your deeper why.

2. Bitesize can be best

Powerful commitments don't have to mean making big changes all in one go. *Make it doable* was some great advice that worked well for me. A question I am sharing with you here was inspired by the work of Nathaniel Branden on self-esteem.[13] It focuses on incremental shifts. For example, if I was 5% more

---

13   N Branden, *Six Pillars of Self-Esteem: The definitive work on self-esteem by the leading pioneer in the field* (Random House USA, 1995)

committed to becoming visible, I would... (fill in the blank). Then go ahead and take that action. Remove the reference here to being visible if that isn't in alignment for you and replace it with whatever you want to be in action on. If 5% feels too scary, start with 1% or 0.00001%. There is no room for judging the percentage. Stay in your own lane and find what is doable for you.

3. Ask *What would I love?*, not *What do I need/have to do?*

When I think of what my mission, goals and ambitions require of me, I like to come at it from the inquiry – what would I love to create? For me, commitments are more powerful when I lean into what I would love. For example, I don't tend to make health goals around being a certain size or a certain weight. Instead, I tend to commit to honouring my values around health. I want longevity, I want quality of life, I want vitality, I want strength. I've cultivated a powerful energy around this, through connecting with that feeling of vitality. Size and weight take care of themselves because I make choices in alignment with my commitment. Of course, I am not an angel – I have pizza and dessert too now and then. I just don't want it all the time because I want longevity and vitality more. Can you hear in my commitments that they are focused on what I would love to create rather than on giving things up or making sacrifices?

Find the thing that inspires you rather than framing it as something you have to give up or sacrifice.

4. Make both being and doing level commitments

Set your intention for how you will show up – the being commitment – and the actions you will take – the doing commitment – and honour them. Am I committed to being kind, or being judgemental? Am I committed to my publishing deadline or watching Netflix?

Some good reminders

Remember what I said about the reptilian part of the brain being hardwired to alert us to danger? Just know that this part will try to shine a light on unhelpful thinking. If we score nine out of ten on an exam, that part of the brain will want to know what one answer we got wrong. Choose instead to keep coming back to the nine you got right. Keep shining a light on the nine. Keep shining a light on the wins to recondition your idea of who you are and what you're capable of. With any evolution, there will be things that don't work out as we hoped. By all means, look at the one you didn't get as well as the nine, but look with love and curiosity, not blame and judgement. There might be growth in there for you, and growth does not require blame. Remember what I said about not attaching that result to your identity.

Remember, this isn't about getting rid of the limiting thoughts completely. We don't need them to be gone if we are relating to them differently. You will find that imposter thinking might pop back up when you think you've said adios to it – these narratives will show up again as we evolve and stretch into new heights. See them as an indicator that you are growing and you are on the right path. Not as a sign that you haven't changed.

Remember to be patient with yourself as you build these new muscles and practise implementing your learning. We all have what I like to call *human moments*. Where we forget who we are and don't show up as our best selves. Practise that value of kindness on yourself, take the learning from it, and keep going. Your journey ahead can be a wonderful one. You will fall off the path – we all do, and that's OK. Love yourself and hop back on.

Words of encouragement

This book and these lessons won't work unless you *do*. I said it at the beginning: the first lesson is about being on the court, playing the game of life, being in the transformation zone and inhibiting your learning. This is an infinite game. You are waking up to an understanding of the human design, and you are now armed with some game-changing life lessons and powerful invitations that, if embodied, can make a real difference in the quality of your future.

AN INVITATION TO... MAKE POWERFUL COMMITMENTS

We unknowingly all put ceilings on our lives. We can't possibly know how great the vantage point is from the penthouse suite if we don't realise we're looking out of the second-floor window. Life might be cracking already; how exponential are you willing to let it get?

Keep coming back to this book again and again, and always read it as an invitation inwards. What are the stories holding up for you to discover about yourself? Let go of the context and instead listen for the principles and insights they point you to. They are relevant for everyone. As we evolve, these lessons land deeper. I can't tell you how much more I get from books the second, third or fourth time I read them. Sometimes years later. Because I have changed, and my listening has evolved. I have become more open, more awake, more conscious, and lessons that weren't available for me previously now land differently. Just like I have found with coaching, this work can serve you for a lifetime if you let it.

ACTIVITY: A loving commitment to your desired future

Take a moment now to bring some further intention to your next chapter – the life you want to create.

- Where in your life are you on autopilot, playing small or letting old stories define you, that it is now time to let go of?

Example: *I've been committed to playing it safe by avoiding challenging conversations that could move my career forward. I release this commitment from today.*

- What are the non-negotiable commitments that your future self would want you to honour?

Example: *I commit to speaking up in meetings because I have valuable contributions to offer and value my voice. I embrace this commitment from today.*

Now make a choice...

- Are you committed to being in the spectator stands or actively playing on the field, where growth happens?
- Will you attach to the victim mindset or step into the power of your creative self?
- Will you cling to your old stories, or are you ready to step into your deeper truth?
- Will you choose your fears, or embrace your mission?
- Will you commit to the familiar that is no longer serving you, or to the authentic self who is ready to be free?

The choice is yours. Honour your word.

Your future is ready to be created!

It's A Wrap!

So here we are – we've landed at the end of the book. You've been taken on a journey inward, to meet the ego mind, the subconscious mind, and your powerful ally. You've learned about the nature of thought, the human operating system, and the influence our relationship to thought has on our realities. If you have engaged with the activities, you will be leaving this book with a new level of awareness about yourself than when you began.

My wish is that this understanding – this knowing that you are not your thoughts, this knowing that feelings are not facts, this knowing that you are the witness, not the thinker – allows you to get some distance from automatic thought patterns. From any unhelpful programming and labels that you may have been influenced by up until now and invites you to surrender any small ideas the personal mind may have been entertaining. I hope that it allows you to accept the invitations to go beyond that mind. Beyond the judgements, and into the truth. The truth of who you are. A whole, capable, powerful creator with the infinite intelligence of the universe within you to co-create with.

As you live from this understanding in your daily life, continue to put the thirteen life lessons into practice. Use the five powerful invitations to new expansive ways of being. Step into being states that elevate and enrich your experience of life. *Be* your future self now. Get on the court in a bigger way and get free from the stands. Whatever that looks like for you. You do *you*, but do it from the truth of *you*, not from the illusion of the personal mind. Familiar is not authentic, remember.

I encourage you to reread the book and revisit the activities as many times as you want. As we evolve, so does our listening, and we can be served by the same lesson and the same activity many times over. As we grow, so can our challenges. If you notice thoughts and feelings creeping back in that you thought you had said adios to, know that this is a good sign. It means you are in a higher level of service to yourself. It means you are on the court. It is a sign of growth. Don't be disheartened – the goal is not to get rid of uncomfortable feelings. The goal is to learn to relate to them differently. Then there is no need for them to be gone.

IT'S A WRAP!

Changing your relationship with thought changes the light you emit out into the world, and the world needs light now more than ever. What would you love to create? What is the mission you care about? What do you want your contribution to be?

The embodiment of the principles and messages in this book is an infinite game. If you want to continue the conversation and bring your highest level of contribution to the world, let's talk. You can find my website at www.lisahoppercoaching.com, and you can connect with me on LinkedIn, Instagram or Facebook.

Acknowledgements

Thanks to my friends and family for loving me exactly as I am and exactly as I am not. To my mum, for showing me what it means to be gentle and kind yet determined and resilient. To my dad, for modelling the power of unwavering love. To my brother, for demonstrating strength in long-term commitments and incremental steps. Also to my Gran, who made the best apple crumble on the planet and ignited in me my sense of adventure and independence. I simply wouldn't be the person I am today without each of you.

Thanks to my incredible clients for daring to dream and for saying yes to yourselves. It is never lost on me how much you show up. The willingness to play at your edges and the willingness to keep going in service of your mission, no matter how scary it might feel at times. I learn and grow so much from being in service to you. I love my work because of you. You make my days so fun and meaningful, and it is a joy to watch you shine your lights.

Thanks to my coaches for the life-changing impact. To Michael Serwa, for setting a high bar and for being unapologetically you. To Aila Hale-Coats, for your gentle, powerful love and encouragement. To Carolyn Freyer-Jones, for your commitment to this profession and for helping me out of a pickle. To Gary Mahler, for the invitation into expansive possibility and the Yaletown coffee conversations. To John Patrick Morgan, for the gift that you are – for seeing me at a time when I really needed to be seen and for setting me free. To Dicken Bettinger, for your wisdom and radiance. The world is kinder and brighter with you in it. To Byron Katie, for a phenomenal nine days in LA, and for inspiring me to rock a stage when I am eighty. To Devon Bandison for your infectious energy, fun and storytelling. To Steve Hardison for the invitation to *be* unleashed, and to Daniel Priestley, for your devotion and contribution to business and entrepreneurship.

Thanks to my incredible beta readers, Claire Kewney, Nick Kewney, Ruth Kudzi, Jesse Lipscombe, Afro Ndiritu and Kate Williams. I loved receiving your notes and comments and hearing about what the book was doing for you. I appreciate you beyond belief – the book would not be what it is today without your honest input.

Thanks to Emma Balk-Phillip for bringing my words to life with brilliant illustrations. Neil White

ACKNOWLEDGEMENTS

and Martin Greig of BackPage, for your guidance and insightful conversations. Emma Loen (hair) and Julie Broadfoot (photography) for your artistry. Thanks to The Social Hub, Glasgow, for providing the space where much of this book was written. Thanks to The Power Zone Peloton community and the Kilted Riders Clan for keeping me active and fit throughout the writing process.

And of course, thanks to Lucy McCarraher, Joe Gregory and the team at Rethink Press for all the support and advice along the way. You have turned me into an author – who knew!

Lisa's 'Little Gems, Big Impact'

- We don't get what we want; we get who we're being.
- This is your opportunity to see expansion in the face of adversity.
- What are you tolerating?
- Given what you are sharing, what would you love to create?
- Allow everything, accommodate little.
- There is what is here, what you think is here, and what you think about what you think is here.
- Don't marry your thoughts with your identity.
- Your judgements of others reflect your judgements of yourself.
- What's the fact, and what's the story?

- The present moment is all we ever have – so *now* is a good time to create.
- Your feelings are a barometer of the clarity of thought you are in. The more intense the feeling, the more your thinking is likely off track.
- Garbage in, garbage out!
- Owners focus on what they want. Victims focus on what they fear. Both are internal inventions.[14]
- If you use the gift of free will to hold on to a negative thought, you will suffer terribly.
- You are only ever one thought away from an entirely different experience.
- What would you choose if you knew you were fully supported by life?
- Today I will judge nothing that occurs.[15]
- Unlearn what you think you know to experience truth.
- There are always costs and consequences to doing nothing.
- What you think of me is not my business.
- If you are not enjoying yourself, know that it has something to do with thought.

---

14 S Chandler, *Reinventing Yourself: How to become the person you've always wanted to be* (The Career Press, 2005)
15 H Schucman et al., *A Course in Miracles* (Viking: The Foundation for Inner Peace, 1976)

The Author

Lisa Hopper (PCC) is a visionary life coach, author, speaker, the founder of the UK School of Coaching and Self-Mastery, and a passionate women's empowerment advocate.

Lisa specialises in disrupting clients' conditioning and mental barriers, empowering them to reinvent themselves and design their next-level life from the inside out. She is passionate about creating a kinder, safer world, where women's voices are heard, their ideas are valued and their contributions shape our future.

Lisa believes that business can be a force for good and actively supports initiatives providing girls' education, clean water and food security to those in need around the world.

Her client base is international and diverse, including corporate executives, business owners, law and finance professionals, health experts, creatives and heart-led coaches.

🌐 www.lisahoppercoaching.com
f www.facebook.com/lisahoppercoaching
📷 @lisa_hopper_coaching
in www.linkedin.com/in/lisa-hopper-coaching

www.ingramcontent.com/pod-product-compliance
Lightning Source LLC
Chambersburg PA
CBHW011956150426
43200CB00018B/2924